Anonymous

Revised Charter of the Village of Geneva

Together with the Laws and Ordinances of the Board of Trustees

Anonymous

Revised Charter of the Village of Geneva
Together with the Laws and Ordinances of the Board of Trustees

ISBN/EAN: 9783337373313

Printed in Europe, USA, Canada, Australia, Japan

Cover: Foto ©Suzi / pixelio.de

More available books at **www.hansebooks.com**

REVISED CHARTER

OF THE

VILLAGE OF GENEVA,

PASSED

BY THE LEGISLATURE OF THE STATE OF NEW YORK, MARCH 3, 1871,

TOGETHER WITH

The Subsequent Amendments

THERETO.

ALSO, OTHER ACTS APPLICABLE TO THE VILLAGE OF GENEVA AND THE OFFICERS THEREOF.

PUBLISHED BY AUTHORITY OF THE BOARD OF TRUSTEES.

GENEVA COURIER STEAM POWER PRESSES.
1891.

The first act of the Legislature of the State of New York in relation to the Village of Geneva, is an act entitled "An Act to vest "certain powers and privileges in the freeholders and inhabitants "in the Village of Geneva, in the County of Ontario," passed April 4th, 1806.

This act was afterwards amended, but there is no record left of any proceedings under these acts, until after the passage of "An Act for the Incorporation of the Village of Geneva in the County of Ontario," passed June 8th, 1812, the record of the first action being as follows:

"At a meeting of the Freeholders and inhabitants of the Village "of Geneva, held at Powell's Hotel in said village, according to the "form of the act in such case made and provided, on the third "Monday in May, in the year of our Lord one thousand eight hun-"dred and thirteen, Abraham Dox, Herman H. Bogert and John "Hall (Trustees of said Village appointed pursuant to the act of "the 4th of April, 1806, and the act amending the same,) being "present did preside as inspectors, the following officers were "elected, to wit:

"Foster Barnard, Herman H. Bogert, Abraham Dox, Samuel "Colt and David Cook, Trustees for 1813. James Rees, Treasurer, "David Hudson, Clerk, Jabez Pease, Collector, David Naglee, "Jonathan Doane and Elnathan Noble, Fire Wardens."

PRESIDENTS

OF THE BOARD OF TRUSTEES

APPOINTED EACH YEAR BY THE BOARD.

1825-6. GEORGE GOUNDRY.
1827-8. RICHARD M. BAYLY.
1829. GEORGE GOUNDRY.
1830. WILLIAM TIPPETTS.
1831. No record of any meeting except Charter Election.
1832-3-4. LANSING B. MISNER.
1835-6. DAVID HUDSON.
1837. WILLIAM W. WATSON, from May 9.
" JOHN L. DOX, from June 5.
1838-9. DAVID HUDSON.
1840. WILLIAM E. SILL.
1841. WILLIAM W. WATSON.
1842. SANFORD R. HALL.
1843. ALFRED A. HOLLY.
1844-5-6-7-8. JOHN M BRADFORD.
1849. LUTHER KELLY.
1850. JOSEPH S. LEWIS.
1851. DAVID S. HALL.
1852. SAMUEL M. MORRISON.
1853-4. THOMAS CRAWFORD.
1855. GEORGE BARKLEY, resigns July 2.
1855-6. GEORGE MERRILL, from July 2, 1855.
1857. CHARLES J. FOLGER.
1858. THOMAS HILLHOUSE.
1859. JOHN M. PAGE.
1860. GEORGE W. NICHOLAS.
1861-2. J. CLARK ROGERS.
1863-4-5. WILLIAM P. HAYWARD.

1866. SIDNEY S. MALLORY.
1867. GEORGE B. DUSINBERRE.
1868. SAMUEL H. VER PLANCK.
1869. SIDNEY S. MALLORY.
1870. JAMES M. SOVERHILL.

PRESIDENTS OF THE VILLAGE

ELECTED AT ANNUAL CHARTER ELECTION, FOR THE TERM OF TWO YEARS.

April 1871 to April 1873.	SAMUEL SOUTHWORTH.
" 1873 " 1875.	GEORGE S. CONOVER.
" 1875 " 1877.	MATTHEW WILSON.
" 1877 " 1879.	GEORGE S. CONOVER.
" 1879 " 1881.	WILLIAM B DUNNING.
" 1881 " 1882.	" " "
" 1882 " 1883.	MATTHEW WILSON, Appointed April 18, 1882.
" 1883 " 1885.	MATTHEW WILSON.
" 1885	STEPHEN H. PARKER, Resigned June 30, 1885.
July 7, 1885 to Feb. 1, 1886.	ROSCOE G. CHASE, Appointed to fill vacancy.
Feb. 1, 1886 to April 1889.	WILLIAM B. DUNNING.
April 1889 to April 1891,	" " "
" 1891 " 1893.	DANIEL F. ATTWOOD.

VILLAGE OFFICERS.

1891.

BOARD OF TRUSTEES

ELECTED AT ANNUAL CHARTER ELECTION.

PRESIDENT OF VILLAGE,

DANIEL F. ATTWOOD. - Term expires April 1893.

TRUSTEES.

1st Ward—

THOMAS W. HAWKINS,	term expires	April	1892.
DE WITT HALLENBECK,	"	"	1893.

2d Ward—

SAMUEL D WILLARD,	"	"	1892.
JAMES R. VANCE,	"	"	1893.

3d Ward—

DANIEL E MOORE,	"	"	1892.
JAMES TANEY.	"	"	1893.

VILLAGE CLERK.

HENRY B. GRAVES, - - term expires April, 1893.

TREASURER.

MONTGOMERY S. SANDFORD,
term expires April, 1892.

COLLECTOR.

WILLIAM H. SANDERS, - term expires April 1892.

ASSESSORS.

DELOS W. COLVIN, - -	term expires	April,	1892.
STEPHEN COURSEY, - -	"	"	1893.
THOMAS HENSON, - - -	"	"	1894.

POLICE JUSTICE.

JOHN M. SMELZER, - - term expires April, 1895.

VILLAGE OFFICERS.

1891.

APPOINTED BY THE BOARD OF TRUSTEES.

Street Commissioner,	CHARLES RUSSELL.
Keeper of Cemeteries,	KELLIS CRUTCHFIELD.
Sealer of Weights & Measures,	JAMES L. TURNER.
Fire Wardens,	The Chief and Assistant Engineers and two persons appointed by each fire company.

FIRE DEPARTMENT.

Chief Engineer,	WILLIAM P. O'MALLEY.
1st Assistant Engineer,	THOMAS COURSEY.
2d " "	JAMES TRACEY.
Kanadesaga Steamer Co., Foreman,	P. HICKEY
Hydrant Hose Co., Foreman,	S. F. DEY.
Chas. J. Folger Hook & Ladder Co., Foreman,	H. S. SNYDER.
Nester Hose Co., Foreman,	CHARLES HENNESSEY.
Ogoyago Hose Co., Foreman,	J. GEO. STACEY.

FIRE WARDENS.

CHIEF AND ASSISTANT ENGINEERS.

TIMOTHY CONNELL.
L. R. TINDELL.
G. S. FAIRFAX.
C. W. FAIRFAX.
S. H. TAYLOR.
C. B. GUILE.
THEO. S. KING.
FRANK BRADLEY.
WM. Mc DONOUGH.
WM. O'DEA.

POLICE COMMISSIONERS.

Chairman—F. O. MASON.
Secretary—P. N. NICHOLAS.
E. A. WALTON.

POLICE.

DANIEL KANE, Chief.
WILLIAM MENSCH,
WILLIAM BEALES,
ELMER E. MERRY,
LAWRENCE KINNEY.

BOARD OF HEALTH.

E. A. WALTON, Pres., T. H. SWEENEY, Sec'y.
W. G. HEMIUP, M. D., D. W. COLVIN,
W. E. STUBBS, Registrar of Vital Statistics.
N. B. COVERT, M.D., Health Officer.
PETER CONOVER, Inspector.

GLENWOOD CEMETERY.

"GENEVA CEMETERY COMMISSIONERS."

Pres't. THOMPSON C. MAXWELL.
S. E. SMITH.
Sec'y. STEPHEN H. PARKER.
WILLIAM B. DUNNING.
J. S. LEWIS.
O. J. C. ROSE.
PHILIP N. NICHOLAS.
THOMAS McBLAIN.
Treas. SAM'L SOUTHWORTH.

AN ACT

TO REVISE AND CONSOLIDATE THE LAWS IN RELATION TO THE VILLAGE OF GENEVA, IN THE COUNTY OF ONTARIO.

Chapter 65, *Laws of New York*, 1871.

Passed March 3, 1871--three-fifths being present.

With the amendments contained in the following Acts:

Chapter 189—Laws of 1872—Passed April 8, 1872.
Chapter 265—Laws of 1873—Passed April 23, 1873.
Chapter 623—Laws of 1874—Passed June 9, 1874.
Chapter 247—Laws of 1875—Passed May 5, 1875.
Chapter 306—Laws of 1877—Passed May 2, 1877.
Chapter 66—Laws of 1879—Passed March 6. 1879.
Chapter 163—Laws of 1882—Passed May 15, 1882.
Chapter 294—Laws of 1886—Passed May 6, 1886.
Chapter 241—Laws of 1888—Passed May 8, 1888.
Chapter 411—Laws of 1889—Passed June 8, 1889.
Chapter 233—Laws of 1891--Passed April 22, 1891.
Act of the Board of Supervisors, passed May 27. 1890, extending village boundaries.

REVISED CHARTER.

The People of the State of New York, represented in Senate and Assembly, do enact as follows:

SECTION 1. The act entitled "An act to amend an act incorporating the village of Geneva, in the county of Ontario, passed May sixth, eighteen hundred and thirty-seven," passed April fourteenth, eighteen hundred and fifty-five, and all acts amendatory thereto, are hereby altered and amended so as to read as follows:

TITLE I.

Boundaries and Civil Divisions.

Chap. 623, laws of 1874.

SECTION 1. The tract of territory at the foot of Seneca lake, comprised within a square, bounded on the east by the new Pre-emption line; on the north by the center of the turnpike road and the center of the road passing in front of the dwelling of Reuben S. Torrey; on the west by the west line of the eight acre lots, and by a continuation thereof in the same direction, until it intersects the said north boundary; on the south by a line running east and west of a distance of one mile south from the south end of the Pulteney or park square in Geneva; together with all the lands heretofore taken by the trustees of the village of Geneva for cemetery purposes, known as Glenwood Cemetery, situate, lying and being south of and adjacent to the said south line above mentioned, shall hereafter be known by the name of the "Village of Geneva," and the territory, together with the inhabitants residing therein, shall be a corporation by the name of "The Trustees of the Village of Geneva," and are hereby declared to be vested with and in possession of all the estate, real and personal, rights, privileges and immuni-

Village boundaries.

Corporate name.

Powers of corporation.

ties which (at the time of the passage of this act) appertain and belong to the said village of Geneva.

Districts.

Chap. 189, laws of 1872.

§ 2. The said village of Geneva is hereby divided into three districts or wards, viz: All that part of said village lying south of the middle line of Seneca street, and such line extended eastward until it intersects the east line of the corporation; the middle line of William street, and such line extended westward until it intersects the west line of the corporation, and the middle line of Main street adjoining said two last lines, shall be district number one. All that part of said village lying north of said district number one and west of the middle line of Genesee street, the middle line of Linden street and the middle line of Castle street adjoining said two last lines, shall be district no two; and all the remainder of said village shall be district number three. After five years, and not oftener than once in five years thereafter, the board of trustees of said village may alter the boundaries, but not the number of said districts, by a two-thirds vote. Such districts as thus altered must be composed of contiguous territory, and must each contain as near as may be the same number of inhabitants, according to the last census, State or national. Notice of such alteration to be at once published in all village papers for at least four weeks, and until thus published such alteration shall not be effected.

First district or ward.

Second district or ward.

Third district or ward.

After five years boundaries may be altered.

Notice of alteration to be published.

BOUNDARIES OF VILLAGE ENLARGED.

Ontario County Board of Supervisors, May 27, 1890.

NO. I.

Resolution to extend boundaries.

A resolution to extend the boundaries of the corporate limits of the Village of Geneva in the county of Ontario, adopted by yeas and nays, at a special meeting of the Board of Supervisors of Ontario County, held May 27, 1890, in pursuance of the provisions of section 33, title 8, chapter 291, laws of 1870, and the acts amendatory thereof, a majority of all the members elected, and Philip N. Nicholas, Supervisor of the town of Geneva, in which Town the Village of Geneva is situate, voting in favor thereof:

Whereas, Petition has been made to the Board by the President and Board of Trustees of the Village of Geneva in the County of Ontario, dated the 26th day of May, 1890, asking that such action may be taken by the Board of Supervisors as will extend the boundaries of the said Village of Geneva along the following proposed line, to wit : Petition of the President and Board.

"Beginning at a point on the Waterloo road where the present north bounds of the Village intersect the new Pre-emption line, running thence north along the said new Pre-emption line 1,008 feet to a point in the center of the highway ; thence in a straight line due west to a point in the center of the Carter road, so called ; thence southerly along the center line of the said Carter road to the center line of North street (being the present north bounds of the corporation); thence westerly along the center line of North street, and the center line of the highway which is the continuation of North street, to the center line of the Castle road at the north-east corner of the New York State Experimental Station ; thence south and east along the center line of said Castle road to the present west bounds of the corporation, at or near the residence of William Smith." Limits of new survey.

And whereas, the said President and Board of Trustees do in said petition pray that the lands included between the aforesaid lines and the present north and west bounds of the corporation may be added to and become part of the Village of Geneva, and that the territory together with the inhabitants residing therein may become part of the corporation known as "The Trustees of the Village of Geneva;" now therefore be it

Resolved, That said petition be and the same is hereby granted, and that the corporate limits of the said Village of Geneva be and the same hereby are extended as and from this date, to wit, the 27th day of May, 1890, so as to include the lands and the inhabitants thereof contained within the lines above described and the present north and west bounds of the corporation Resolution to adopt.

Resolved, That the foregoing be entered in full in the minutes of the proceedings of this Board, and that the Clerk furnish the Board of Trustees of the Village of Geneva with a certified copy thereof.

The foregoing resolution was adopted by the Board of Supervisors of the County of Ontario this 27th day of May, 1890, fifteen supervisors, being more than two-thirds of the number elected to said Board, and also the Supervisor of the Town of Geneva voting in favor thereof. Date of adoption.

PHILIP N. NICHOLAS,
Chairman.

HIRAM METCALF,
Clerk.

Clerk's affidavit.

STATE OF NEW YORK, }
COUNTY OF ONTARIO, } ss.

I do hereby certify that I have compared the preceding with the original thereof, on file in my office, and that the same is a correct transcript therefrom and of the whole of said original.

Given under my hand and official seal at Canandaigua
[L. S.] in said County, this 29th day of May, A. D. 1890.

HIRAM METCALF.
Supervisors' Clerk.

TITLE II.

Of the Village Officers, their Election and Appointment.

Village officers.

SECTION 1. The officers of the corporation shall be:

1. A president of the village.

2. Six trustees, two of whom shall reside in each district,

Chap. 189, laws of 1872.

but this shall not apply to trustees in office, when this act takes effect.

3. A clerk.

4. A treasurer.

5. A police justice.

6. A collector.

7. A street commissioner.

8. Three assessors.

9. A police constable, and as many extra police and night watchmen as the board of trustees may appoint.

10. Three fire wardens.

11. One pound master, and such other appointive officers as shall be authorized by this act.

Officers to be Elected or Appointed.

Elective officers.

§ 2. The president, six trustees, three assessors, clerk, collector, treasurer, and police justice, shall be elected as hereinafter provided, by the people of the corporation qualified to vote at the annual state election. The board of trustees shall appoint the police constable, and all extra police and night watchmen.

Officers appointed.

Fire wardens, street commissioner, pound master and such other officers as may be hereinafter provided, and all and every of said

May be removed.

officers thus appointed, may be removed by said board

of trustees at their pleasure. The police justice shall be subject to removal by the county judge of Ontario county on written charges after a trial on notice. Every officer, whether elected or appointed, must be and at all times continue to be a resident and elector of the village and district for which he is chosen, otherwise his office is vacant, and the board of trustees must so declare and provide for a new election or appointment.

County Judge may remove Police Justice for cause.

Officers must be residents of village.

Time and Manner of Election.

Chap. 189, laws of 1872.

§ 3. An election of the elective officers of this corporation shall be held annually on the first Monday of April,* at such place in each district as shall be designated by the board of trustees, and fifteen days' notice shall be given of said election and the places of holding the same, by publishing the same in all the newspapers of the village; provided, however, that notices of the places of election for the year eighteen hundred and seventy-two may be by one insertion in one of the village papers.

Annual election.

Notice.

§ 4. There shall be an election poll in each of said three districts. Such members or any member of the board of trustees as shall be present shall preside at such polls and elections. In case no member of the board of trustees shall be present at any poll at the hour appointed for its opening, the electors of said district there assembled may appoint a chairman to preside. The presiding officer or officers at such elections are hereby authorized to preserve order, judge of the qualifications of the electors, canvass the votes and make the returns as specified by this act; and all powers granted to inspectors of election by the election laws of this State, are hereby conferred upon them for the purposes of such charter elections. The polls of said election shall each be open at nine o'clock, A.M., and shall continue open without intermission until four o'clock in the afternoon, when they shall be closed.* There shall be two ballot boxes at each poll, the one labeled "village," the other labeled "ward." Each voter shall vote in the ward or district in which he resides at the time of offering his vote. Each voter may

The election polls.

Elections, how conducted.

Ballot boxes, "ward" and "village."

Voters to be resident of district.

vote two tickets: the one of said tickets shall contain the names of all the village officers elected at such election, for whom the elector offering the vote desires to vote, except the trustee for that district. The other of said tickets shall have the name of the trustee for that district for whom the elector may desire to vote. Each trustee can only be voted for by the electors resident in his district, and the trustee receiving the largest number of the votes for trustee cast in his district shall be thereby elected. All other village officers receiving the highest number of votes cast for that office in all three districts shall be declared elected. Said ticket may be written or printed, or partly written and partly printed, and shall state the office for which, and the name of the person for whom the elector desires to vote. The one containing the name of the trustee for that district shall be labeled "ward," and shall be deposited in the ballot box labeled "ward." The other ticket shall be labeled "village," and shall be deposited in the ballot box labeled "village." Immediately on closing said polls the presiding officer or officers at each of said polls shall forthwith, without adjourning, canvass the votes cast at such election at that poll, and shall make and certify two complete and accurate statements thereof, and forthwith file one of such statements with the clerk of said village and the other with the clerk of the county of Ontario. On the next day after any election, the board of trustees of said village shall convene as a board of canvassers, at two o'clock P.M., and proceed to examine said statements or returns of said election held the day before, and from such statements and returns they shall determine and decide who were elected officers of the village at such election, as hereinbefore provided. In making such determination they shall allow each candidate any vote that it is apparent was intended for him, although the name may be mis-spelled or not fully written out. The clerk of the village shall thereupon enter at large upon the records of said village, the said statements and returns and the decision of the board of trustees thereupon, and file the original state-

Trustees, how voted for.

Ballots.

Canvass.

Duty of clerk.

ments in his office and notify the persons thus declared and decided elected of their election.

*Sections 3 and 4 above are essentially modified by the following act:

CHAP. 247

AN ACT in relation to the election of village officers in Geneva, Ontario County, passed May 5, 1875, three-fifths being present.

As amended by Chap. 66, passed March 6, 1879, three-fifths being present.

The People of the State of New York, represented in the Senate and Assembly, do enact as follows:

SECTION 1. Hereafter the election of all officers to be chosen by the electors under the charter of, the village of Geneva, Ontario County, shall be held on the first Monday of February in each year, and the several polls for such election shall be open at eight o'clock in the morning, and continue open without intermission until sundown, when they shall be closed. But nothing in this act shall be construed so as to affect the tenure of office of the elective officers of the said village of Geneva; but the terms of said officers shall begin on the first Monday in April next after the election. Time of annual election. Time of opening and closing polls.

§ 2. This act shall take effect immediately.

Election of President and Trustees.

§ 5. At the first election [first Monday in April eighteen hundred and seventy-one] the president and all other elective officers and all six trustees shall be elected; the president and the trustees from the second, fourth and sixth districts for the full term of two years, and the trustees from the first, third and fifth districts for only one year, and at each annual village election after the first, there shall be elected, alternately, first, the trustees from the first, third and fifth districts, and the next year the president and trustees from the second and fourth and sixth districts, and after the first election all trustees shall hold their office for the full term of two pears. But after the passage of this act, one trustee shall be elected by the electors of each district each year as in this act provided. First election and terms of officers. **Chap. 189, laws of 1872.** One trustee in each district.

Election of Assessors.

Terms of office of assessors. § 6. At the first election under this charter there shall be elected all three assessors, one for one year, one for two years and one for the full term of three years, to be specified on the ballot: at each annual village election after the first, only one assessor shall be elected, to hold for the full term of three years.

Officers must take Oath of Office

Oath of office. § 7. Every officer of this village whether elected or appointed shall, before entering upon the duties of his office, take and file with the clerk the oath of office prescribed by the constitution.

Certain Officers must file Bonds.

Bonds to be filed. § 8. The treasurer, collector, police justice, police constable and such other officers as may be required by the board of trustees shall, severally, before they or either of them, respectively, enter upon the duties of their respective offices, execute and file with the clerk a bond to the village of Geneva, in such sum, and with two or more sureties (who shall each justify in the usual form to double the amount of the bond) as the board of trustees, or a majority thereof, shall, in writing thereon approve, conditioned that he or they will faithfully execute and discharge each and every of the duties of his or their office, and will, on demand of the president of the village or board of trustees, or by vote of any village meeting, duly account for and pay over all moneys received by him or them, or that may in any way come to his or their hands on account of his or their official capacity, and no such officer shall be entitled to any salary, pay or fees until he shall have given and filed said bond as herein required.

Condition.

Neglect to take Oath or File Bond, Consequences of

Neglect to take oath. § 9. If any officer of this village, either elected or appointed, shall neglect or fail to take and file the constitutional oath of office as hereinbefore required, within ten days after he shall be personally notified by the clerk of his election or appointment, or if any officer who, by this charter or by the board of trustees as herein provided, shall be required to make and file a bond, shall fail to make and file his bond duly approved as by this charter required, within thirty days after such personal notice, in either case the said officer thus failing to file such oath or make and file his bond, shall be deemed to have declined the office, and his place shall be filled as in case of a vacancy. And for such failure the board of trustees may impose a fine not to exceed fifty dollars.

Or file bond.

To work vacancy.

Penalty.

Vacancies, How Filled.

§ 10. All vacancies in any village office, except elective offices, may be filled by appointment as herein provided by the board of trustees. If any vacancy occur in any elective office, the board of trustees may, by appointment, fill the same until the next annual village election, and if the time of office of such vacancy shall not then end, there shall be elected at such election some person to fill the balance of such vacancy, to be so designated on the ballot.

Vacancies.

Mode and Proof of Appointment.

§ 11. All appointments or nominations by the board of trustees shall be in writing, signed by the members making the appointment, and the clerk shall duly enter in full in the records such written appointment or nomination. The certificate of such appointment or election, duly signed by the clerk, and sealed with the corporate seal, shall be prima facie evidence of such appointment or election in all courts or elsewhere in this state. And the clerk shall file in the county clerk's office of Ontario county a certified copy of all appointments of police constable, or extra police or night watchmen, and also a certificate of the removal of any of them whenever any are removed from office.

Appointments or nominations must be in writing.

Certificate.

Appointments of police officers how filed.

TITLE III.

OF THE BOARD OF TRUSTEES.

Organization.

Board of trustees, how formed.

SECTION 1. The board of trustees shall consist of the president and six trustees. The president shall preside; he shall vote, the same as any other member of the board. The board may elect one of its number to preside in the absence of the president. It shall require at least four members of the board to constitute a quorum for the transaction of any business.

President.

Business quorum of board.

Stated and Special Meetings.

Stated meetings.

§ 2. The board of trustees shall hold stated meetings on the third Tuesday of each month, at seven o'clock, P.M., and such others as they may by by-law appoint. They may also hold special meetings, to be called by the president or any two trustees, by written notice delivered personally or left at the residence of each member of the board. All such meetings, both stated and special, shall be held at such place as the board of trustees shall by by-law appoint, and shall at all times be public and open to any taxable inhabitant of this corporation, except at such times as the board may have under consideration the appointment, nomination or removal of any village officer, or member of the fire department, subject to removal by said board and at such times it may exclude every person but the clerk from its session. Within two days after each meeting of the board of trustees the clerk shall prepare a full, concise and accurate, but brief statement of the various votes, accounts audited, stating the amount, persons for whom, and for what audited, and proceedings of said board, and shall furnish a copy of the same for each, not exceeding two, village papers, and cause said statement to be published in such papers, provided, however, that the expense for such publication

Special meetings, how called.

Where to be held.

To be public.

Exception.

Chap. 189, laws of 1872.

Statement to be made by clerk

shall not exceed one hundred dollars yearly for each paper in which said proceedings are published, and provided, further, the village tax meeting vote the money for that purpose.

Powers and Duties of the Board of Trustees.

§ 3. The said board of trustees shall have the management and control of the finances, and all the property, real and personal, belonging to the said corporation, subject to the provisions and restrictions of this act; and shall examine, settle and audit all accounts against the village, of its officers or others. They are authorized, within the limits of said village, **Trustees to have control of finances.** **Their powers and duties.**

1. To prevent vice and immorality; to preserve peace and good order; to prevent and quell riots and disorderly assemblages. **Prevention of vice.**

2. To appoint, select or nominate all officers or employees of this village, not made elective by this act. To fix and determine the salary, pay or fees of all officers or employees of this village, not otherwise provided for by this act; and to raise, by tax, the salary of all officers of said village; but said board of trustees or any member thereof shall not receive any salary, pay or emolument whatever. **Appointment of non-elective officers.** **Fixing and raising salary. Trustees to receive no pay.**

3. To restrain and suppress disorderly and gaming-houses, all instruments and devices used for gaming, and to prohibit all gaming and fraudulent devices within the said village. **To suppress disorderly and gaming houses.**

4. To regulate and fix the hours of closing saloons, shops and places in which intoxicating liquors are sold. **Regulating closing of liquor saloons.**

5. To restrain and regulate all exhibitions of any natural or artificial curiosities, caravans of animals, theatrical and other shows and exhibitions, circuses or other performances for money, and authorize the same, on such terms as the board of trustees shall deem expedient. **Licensing exhibitions, shows, etc.**

6. To repress and restrain houses of ill-fame, billiard tables, bowling alleys and pistol galleries. **Houses of ill-fame, bowling alleys, etc.**

Abatement of nuisances.

Cleansing of soap factories, tanneries, etc.

7. To provide for the abatement of nuisances: to compel the owners or occupants of any grocery, tallow-chandler shop, soap factory, tanning stall, privy or sewer, or other unwholesome or nauseous house or thing, or place, to clease, remove or abate the same, from time to time, as often as in the opinion of the board of trustees the same may be necessary for the health and comfort and convenience of the inhabitants of said village: and said trustees shall have full power to enter upon the premises upon which a nuisance is situated, and cause the same to be removed, and cause the expenses thereof to be assessed upon and collected from the premises on which the same is situated, and may also enforce the penalty imposed by the ordinance of said village for erecting or maintaining such nuisance; but all such determinations shall require a concurring vote of two-thirds of all the trustees of said village.

Powers to remove or abate the same.

Expense of removal, how assessed.

Restriction.

Location of slaughter houses, etc.

Regulating keeping of gunpowder, etc.

8 To direct the location of all slaughter-houses, markets, and houses for storing gunpowder, or any combustible substance, and to regulate the keeping and conveying of gunpowder and other dangerous materials, and the use of candles and lights in barns, stables and other buildings.

Fireworks and gunpowder.

9. To prohibit and regulate the exhibition of fireworks, the storing and sale of gunpowder, and the discharge of firearms within said village.

Providing for drainage.

10. To provide for the proper drainage of said village, and to that end to erect, maintain or repair all necessary drains in the streets or public grounds of said village and to regulate and direct, by by-law or resolution, the mode, manner and time in which all private drains shall be made, maintained or repaired; and, in case of neglect or refusal to make, maintain or repair any private drain as directed, to enforce the same by fine, by doing the work or otherwise.

Preventing horse racing, etc.

11. To prevent horse racing, immoderate driving in the streets of said village, and to authorize the stopping of any one who shall be guilty of immoderate riding or driving in said streets, by any person; and to prevent

the flying of kites, rolling hoops, playing at ball, sliding down hill on sleds, or any other amusements practiced, having a tendency to endanger or annoy persons passing on the streets or sidewalks, or to frighten teams or horses in said village. Flying of kites, rolling hoops, playing ball, etc.

12. To prevent the incumbering of the streets, squares, sidewalks, crosswalks, lanes and alleys with teams, carriages, carts, sleighs, sleds, wheelbarrows, boxes, lumber, timber, firewood, coal or any other substance or material whatsoever. Preventing obstruction of streets.

13. To prevent or regulate the erection or construction of any projection from or in front of any building, in over or upon any of the streets or sidewalks in said village, and cause the same to be removed at the expense of the owner or occupant of the premises. Regulating the construction of awnings,

14. To prohibit any person from bringing and depositing, within the limit of said village, any dead carcass or other unwholesome or offensive substance; and to require the removal or destruction, by any person who shall leave on or upon his premises any such substances, or any putrid meats, fish, hides or skins, of any kind, and on his default, the removal or destruction thereof by some officer of the village; the expense thereof to be paid by the person or persons violating any such prohibition, or refusing or neglecting to make such removal or destruction. Prohibiting offensive substances.

15. To require the removal from said village of all persons having infectious or pestilential diseases, and to authorize and require any officer of said village to remove such person. Removal of diseased persons.

16. To direct the keeping and returning of bills of mortality. Keeping of bills of mortality.

17. To appoint not exceeding five tax-payers of said village to serve as health commissioners, one of whom shall be designated by such board of trustees as presiding officer thereof, and shall constitute a board of health of said village, and said board of health shall have all the powers and be subject to all the duties of "An act for the preservation of public health," passed April tenth, **Chap. 306, laws of 1877.** Appointment of board of health. Its powers and duties.

eighteen hundred and fifty, in addition to the powers which are conferred or may be authorized by this act.

Prevention of pestilential diseases.

18. To take such measures as they shall deem effectual to prevent the entrance of any pestilential or infectious diseases in the village.

Regulation of bathing.

19. To regulate and determine the time and place of bathing and swimming in the waters of said village.

Running at large of animals.

20. To restrain the running at large of cattle, horses, swine or other animals, and to authorize the impounding and sale of the same for the penalty and costs of keeping and proceedings, and for this purpose to erect and maintain a public pound, and make all necessary rules for the maintenance and regulation thereof, and impose such penalties, costs, charges and expenses upon the owners of animals impounded therein as they may deem best, and regulate the mode and manner of sale thereof as aforesaid; and to impose suitable and proper penalties for any injury to, or destruction of, such pound, or any forcible or unlawful rescue or removal of animals impounded therein.

Public pound.

Cleaning of side walks.

21. To require all persons owning or occupying property in said village, and the owners of unoccupied property therein, to remove all snow and dirt from the sidewalks in front of the premises so owned or occupied by them, and to keep the same clean and free therefrom, and, in case of neglect or refusal on the part of such owner or occupant, to remove the same at his expense, and impose and collect such penalty as shall be provided by any ordinance of said corporation for such neglect or refusal.

Expense, how collected.

Ringing of bells, etc.

22. To regulate the ringing of bells, and the crying of goods, wares and merchandise, or other commodity in the said village.

Regulating of lotteries and auctions.

23. To prohibit, restrain and regulate all gift enterprises, or sales of goods founded upon or connected with any gift, lottery or chance, in said village, and to restrain and regulate auctioneering in said village, and prohibit and regulate the hawking, peddling, auctioneering or sale of property in the streets, alleys, lanes or public parks of said village.

Hawking, peddling.

24. To prevent and regulate the running at large of dogs in said village, and to authorize the destruction of the same. Dogs running at large.

25. To establish, regulate, make and guard public reservoirs, pumps and wells, and to provide for supplying the village with water by means of pipes, and to make regulations in regard to the use of the same. Public reservoirs and water works.

26. To appoint one or more sealers of weights and measures. Appointment of sealers of weights and measures.

27 To provide for keeping and regulating hay scales, and to establish, order and regulate markets, and to regulate the vending of wood, meats, vegetables, hay, fruit, fish and provisions of all kinds. Regulation of markets, hay scales, sale of wood, meats, etc.

28. To erect, maintain and repair all engine-houses, lock-up, jail, town-house or other public building necessary for the corporation. To aid in the erection of any public building which it shall be necessary to occupy in part or wholly for the business of said village or its officers, or to lease any building or premises for the same purpose; but no such work shall be entered upon or contract entered into until the money to pay for the same is voted therefor by the village at a tax meeting, as hereinafter provided; and all work, except repairing, shall be done by contract, to be publicly advertised and let to the lowest responsible bidder, giving good security for the faithful performance of said work. Engine houses and public buildings. Not to be created until money is voted. Work to be done by contract.

29. To open, improve, regulate, repair and control all streets and highways in said willage. To establish, regulate and maintain public parks in said village, and to make all necessary rules for the mode or manner of use or occupation, preservation, protection or adornment of said streets or public parks, and to that end to plant, cultivate, protect, trim and preserve shade trees in said village. Streets and parks.

For the purpose of supplying the village with water, the board of trustees are hereby authorized to enter into a contract with the Geneva water works company or any other corporation, for the laying down of pipes, erection of hydrants and other necessary fixtures in said village to **Chap. 189, laws of 1872.** May contract for supply of water.

accomplish said purpose, and, in consideration therefor, agree to pay a certain sum in the aggregate or a certain sum annually on such conditions and in such manner as by said contract shall be provided. But said contract shall not take effect unless the same shall be approved by a vote of the tax-payers of said village, to be taken at a special election as provided by section twelve of title six of the act hereby amended. A full copy of said contract shall be published, and said election shall be conducted in all respects as provided by said section twelve, except the votes shall be, "for the contract" or "against the contract," and said contract may be for any number of years more than three, and if approved shall be effectual for the time as therein provided. If the majority of said votes cast at such election are "for the contract," then the said contract shall be valid. The board of trustees may levy and collect the amount agreed to be paid annually as an annual tax, as other taxes are levied and collected. But in case of an agreement to pay an aggregate amount, such sum shall not exceed thirty thousand dollars, to be provided as is limited in said section twelve of title six of the act hereby amended.

Contract to be approved by vote.

Vote how taken.

Chap. 294, laws of 1886.

Lighting of streets.

30. To provide for lighting the streets and public places in the village, the board of trustees are hereby authorized and empowered to enter into a contract with any person, or persons or corporations (competent to do said work), for the erection of poles, wires, lamp-posts or other necessary fixtures in said village to accomplish said purpose, and, in consideration therefor, agree to pay a certain sum in the aggregate or a certain sum annually on such conditions and in such manner as by said contract shall be provided. But said contract shall not take effect unless the same shall be approved by a vote of the tax-payers of said village, to be taken at a special election, as provided by section twelve of title six of the act hereby amended. A full copy of said contract shall be published, and said election shall be conducted in all respects as provided by said section twelve, except the votes shall be "for the contract," or "against the contract," and said contract may

Trustees may contract, subject to vote of taxpayers.

be for any number of years not more than ten, and if approved shall be effectual for the time as therein provided If the majority of said votes cast at such election are "for the contract," then the said contract shall be valid. The board of trustees may levy and collect the amount agreed to be paid annually as an annual tax, as other taxes are levied and collected. But in case of an agreement to pay an aggregate amount, such sum shall not exceed thirty thousand dollars, to be provided as is limited in said section twelve of title six of the act hereby amended.

Limitation of aggregate amount.

31. To prescribe the powers and duties of the treasurer, clerk, street commissioner, pound-master, fire-wardens and all officers appointed by the board of trustees.

To prescribe duties of officers.

32. To organize and establish a fire department, (either paid or unpaid); to divide the same into divisions or companies; to determine the number of members of each and all of said companies or divisions, and their duties and powers respectively; to determine as to the officers of said divisions or companies, and their duties and powers respectively; to chose or select all members of said fire department or provide for their choice or selection; to appoint or provide for the choice of all officers of said fire department or any of the divisions or companies thereof; to direct or designate what engine, either steamer or hand, or what apparatus, either hose, ladders, hooks, buckets or any other, each of said divisions or companies, or each of said officers of said fire department or companies, or each of the members, or any designated number of them, shall respectively take possession of, use and be responsible for; and how they or either of them shall respectively take possession of or use the same, and to what extent they or either of them shall be responsible for the same: to take exclusive possession of, control, manage and repair all engines, hose, ladders, hooks, buckets, or other implements or accoutrements now owned or controlled by the said village of Geneva, or the trustees thereof, and to purchase any other engine (steamer or hand), hose, horses, harness, ladders, hooks, buckets, or other implements, accoutrements or material necessary for the proper and efficient

Fire department.

Officers and members, how chosen.

Apparatus, how assigned.

And to be under the control of the trustees.

Trustees to fix pay of firemen, etc.

operation of said fire department, or any company, division, officer or member thereof; to determine the pay (if any), and mode of payment of all officers and members of said fire department: to remove or dismiss any members or officer of said fire department at their pleasure, or to provide how and in what manner and for what cause any officer or member of said fire deparment may be removed or dismissed; to provide by by-law what penalty or fine any officer or member of the fire department may forfeit or be subjected to for any violation of any of the rules or regulations of said board of trustees, or for any disobedience, refual or neglect to obey the orders of any member of said board of trustees, or of any superior in said fire department; and generally to make such fire laws, rules, regulations or ordinances relating to said fire department, and the rights and duties of the same, or of any of the officers or members therof, and relative to the duties of all peasons or citizens during fires in said village as they may deem best, and to enforce the same by suitable and proper penalties; and to do or cause to be done any and every thing necessary and proper to protect the property in said village from injury or destruction by fire; provided, always, all such by-laws, rules and regulations are not inconsistent with or contrary to the constitution or laws of this state, or of the United States. But the said board of trustees shall enter into no contract nor make any purchase, unless the money to pay therefor has been legally voted at a village meeting.

Firemen subject to penalty.

General powers in regard to fire laws.

Restriction.

Debts not to be incurred.

Chap. 306, laws of 1877.

Protection of property at fires.

33. To protect property, both real and personal, of individuals at times of fires, and to appoint guards for the protection of the same, and to prescribe their powers and compensation. To establish, by ordinance, fire limits within said village of Geneva, within which limits no building or structure of wood shall be erected, or addition of wood be made to any building or structure now erected, and to regulate the erection of buildings and structures with in such limits, and the materials thereof, and may require iron shutters to be placed on the outer doors and windows of buildings and structures already erected, and upon such as

Fire limits.

Regulations for erection of buildings.

shall be constructed: and any person who shall violate any such ordinance or regulation, shall forfeit to said village of Geneva, the sum of two hundred and fifty dollars; and every building or structure erected contrary to said ordinance, is hereby declared to be a common nuisance, and may be abated and removed as such by the board of trustees.

Penalties.

Nuisances.

34. To authorize the fire wardens, at reasonable times, to enter and examine all houses, stores, yards and outbuildings, to ascertain if they are in a dangerous state in regard to fires, and direct or compel the owner or occupant to put the same in a safe condition, and in default, to appoint any person to do the same at the expense of such owner or occupant.

Fire wardens may enter and examine dangerous buildings.

35. To regulate and control the use of all engine-houses, rooms and buildings owned or occupied by said village of Geneva, and cause such of them, and the property therein, belonging to said village, to be insured as they shall deem best.

Control and insurance of engine houses, etc.

36. To establish, maintain, lay out, cultivate, adorn and take care of a cemetery, and regulate the burial of the dead therein, within or near by this corporation, or to aid others in establishing and maintaining such cemetery, provided this corporation shall own and have the benefit of a proper portion of such cemetery, and to take care of, cultivate and adorn, and regulate the burial of the dead in all cemeteries now owned or controlled by this corporation, and for such purposes to plant and cultivate trees or shrubs, and to lay out, make and keep in repair, roads and walks through the same, and to appoint a cemetery keeper to take charge of the same.

Cemeteries, and burial of dead.

37. To purchase, hold, sell, convey and agree to purchase and convey real estate whenever necessary or expedient for the accomplishment or execution of any of the purposes, or powers or duties mentioned in this act.

Purchase and sale of real estate.

38. To cause the sidewalks on the streets and highways in said village to be leveled, raised, planked, graded, paved, flagged and repaired, and ornamented with trees, by

Sidewalks.

and at the expense of the owners or occupants of the lands and premises benefitted thereby; and, if not done by such owners or occupants in such manner, and of the material and kind, and within the time, prescribed by the board of trustees, the said board of trustees may make such improvements and repairs, and assess and collect the expense thereof upon such owners or occupants in the manner hereinafter in this act provided.

Gas and water companies laying pipes in streets.

39. To provide by by-law when, how, and in what manner any gas or water company, or any of their officers or employees, or any other person or corporation not now authorized by law to do the same, may disturb, dig up, or in any way interfere with, the streets of said village or any portion of the materials or soil thereof. And when, how, and in what manner, and on what conditions except as now permitted by law, they may lay pipes, drains or any other thing or material on or under the surface of any of said streets or public grounds of said village; and to prohibit any interference with said streets or public grounds of said village, or the laying of any pipes or drains, or other material or thing, on or under the surface of said streets or public grounds, except authorized by law as aforesaid, unless in accordance with said by-laws thus made, and to enforce by proper penalty any violation or attempt to violate said by-laws.

By-laws, ordinances, other powers.

40. To make such other general ordinances, by-laws and regulations, not repugnant to the general laws of the state, as they shall deem expedient for the good government of the village.

Enforcement of by-laws and ordinances, etc.

41. For the purposes aforesaid, or any of them, or of executing any other powers conferred upon them by this act, to make, establish and publish, modify, ammend and repeal ordinances, rules and regulations and by-laws, to prescribe such penalties and fines as they may deem proper for the violation of them, not exceeding fifty dollars for any one offense, except as herein otherwise provided, and to collect the same of any persons guilty of such violation, in any court having jurisdiction of such cases; or in case any person or corporation refuse or neglect to do any act

To prescribe penalties.

or work as thereunto required, to do or procure the same to be done, and collect the cost and expense of the same as a fine or penalty, or as a tax, or as both, in the same manner as any other fine or penalty, or any tax, is provided to be collected by this act; but all such rules, ordinances, regulations and by-laws shall be published once in each week, for two weeks successively, in one or more newspapers published in said village, before they shall take effect.

Publication of by-laws, ordinances, etc.

Suits for Forfeitures.

§ 4. All proceedings or actions to recover or enforce any penalty or forfeiture incurred under this act, or the ordinances, by-laws, rules, orders or regulations made by authority or in pursuance thereof, may be had and taken before the police justice of this village, or before or by any court of civil jurisdiction, in accordance with the rules thereof, within this state; and the said police justice or court shall have jurisdiction to hear, try and determine the same, and render judgment therein, and in any such action or proceedings, brought before the police justice of this village, the first process may be by warrant, and, on judgment being recovered for any such penalty, execution shall issue against the person of the defendant, as well as against his property, in the same manner as in actions for torts. In any such action or proceeding, the certificate of the clerk of said village of Geneva, under the corporate seal of said village, setting forth any such ordinance, by-law, rule or regulation, and certifying the adoption of the same, and the date of such adoption by the board of trustees of said village, and the fact of the publication thereof, shall be presumptive evidence of the existence and due passage or adoption of any such ordinance, by-law, rule or regulation, and the due publication thereof, according to the requirements of this act.

Actions to enforce penalties. How brought.

Jurisdiction of Police Justice.

Executions, how issued.

By-laws, ordinances, etc., how read in evidence.

TITLE IV.

OFFICERS OF THE VILLAGE—THEIR POWERS, DUTIES, TERM OF OFFICE, AND SALARIES OR FEES.

The President.

Term of office, powers and duties.

SECTION 1. The president shall hold his office for two years. It shall be his duty to preside, when present, at all meetings of the board of trustees; to see that this charter and all its by-laws and ordinances are strictly enforced, and the fines imposed thereby promptly collected; to see that all officers of this village perform all

To be Chief of Police.

their duties, and to preserve order; and to that end he shall be chief of the police, and the police constable and all extra policemen or night watchmen shall be subject to and obey all his orders and directions.

The Clerk.

Terms of office, powers and duties.

§ 2. The clerk shall hold his office for two years. It shall be his duty to attend all meetings of the people on the business of the corporation; to attend all meetings of the board of trustees; to record all their proceedings, and, in case of appointment or nomination of any officer, to

Chap. 233, laws of 1891.

record such appointment in full, stating the names of the members of the board who voted for the same. He shall also record all bonds of village officers at length, including the justification and approval indorsed thereon. He shall also enter at length all resolutions or ordinances adopted by said board, stating the names of those members of the board who voted for the same. It shall be his duty to keep all books, records, deeds and writings belonging to the corporation, and deliver the same to his successor on demand, and to perform any other duties that the board

Salary.

of trustees may by by-laws or ordinances require. His salary shall be three hundred dollars yearly, and he shall receive no other compensation, fee or emolument.

The Treasurer

§ 3. The treasurer shall receive all moneys directed to be paid into the treasury, and shall pay out the same on the warrant or order of the president, or presiding officer, countersigned by the clerk or secretary; he shall, at each annual election, exhibit an account showing the state of the treasury, and the several sums of money which shall have been received and paid out by him during the preceding year; and shall deliver to his successor in office, on receiving five day's notice to that effect, all the moneys, books and papers appertaining to his office. And all the vouchers for moneys paid out by the treasurer during the year preceding the annual tax meeting, shall be by him, within five days after the adjournment of such tax meeting, delivered to the board of trustees, who shall cause the same to be filed in their office.

Duties.

Annual financial report.

Chap. 623, laws of 1874. Vouchers to be delivered to trustees.

Collector.

§ 4. The collector shall collect all moneys which shall be ordered by the corporation to be raised by tax, and which shall be specified in any tax list furnished to him at the time by the board of trustees, or a majority of them, signed by a majority of them; and he is authorized to exercise the same powers and to pursue the same remedies in the collection of taxes as by law are given to the collectors in the several towns of this state. His fees shall be fixed by the voters at the annual village tax meeting, but they shall not exceed those of town collector.

Duties and powers.

Fees.

Street Commissioner.

§ 5. The street commissioner shall hold his office during the pleasure of the board of trustees. His salary or pay shall be fixed by the board of trustees. It shall be his duty to see that the streets and public parks of the village are kept in good repair; that all ordinances and by-laws with regard to the streets and public parks are duly enforced and obeyed. Subject to the direction of the board

Term, salary and duties.

of trustees, he shall superintend and see that all work upon the streets of this village is properly done, and that all employees working upon the streets do their duty; and he shall perform such other duties as the board of trustees may by law direct.

Assessors.

Duties and powers.

§ 6. The assessors shall make out and deliver to the board of trustees valuations of estates, real and personal, assessments and assessment rolls, with apportionment of taxes annexed thereto, whenever they shall be required by the trustees to do so, and as herein provided; and in making such assessment they shall be guided by the same principles of valuation as prescribed by law for assessors of towns.

Sealers of Weights and Measures.

Term of office and powers.

§ 7. The sealer of weights and measures shall hold his office for two years unless sooner removed. He shall have the same powers, and be subject to the same rules and restrictions, as sealers of weights and measures in the towns. The sealer of weights and measures of Ontario county shall furnish him, when ordered by the board of trustees, a copy of the standards of the weights and measures of this state, at the expense of this village. His fees, and the mode of collection or payment, shall be determined by the board of trustees, subject to the laws of this state as to sealers of weights and measures in towns; he shall obey all orders and be under the direction of the board of trustees. No other sealer of weights and measures shall perform any of the duties of his office within this corporation, unless it be supervisory, and for such services he shall collect no fees from any inhabitant of this village.

Standard of weights and measures.

Fees.

Other Officers.

Duties and salaries.

§ 8. The fire warden, cemetery keeper, pound master, wood inspector and all other officers, shall perform such duties as shall be required of them by the by-laws of this corporation. Their salary, pay or fees, and the mode of payment and collection of the same, shall be fixed by the board of trustees by their by-laws; but the salaries of all the officers of this village (except the police justice and clerk) which are payable out of the village treasury, shall not exceed in the aggregate the sum of one thousand dollars in one year, unless a greater amount be allowed and voted at the annual tax meeting.

Restriction on amount of salaries.

Fire Department.

§ 9. All officers of the fire department shall be chosen by the board of trustees, or in such manner as they may by by-law direct. Their term of office shall be at the pleasure of the board of trustees, or for such term as they may by by-law prescribe. There shall be a chief engineer of the fire department, a fireman and engineer for each steam engine company, a foreman for each other fire or hook-and-ladder company, and such additional or other officers as the by-laws shall prescribe. The board of trustees shall determine whether the officers or members of the fire department shall be paid or not, and if paid, what amount, and how they shall be paid; but all proposed expenses of the fire department must be submitted to, and voted upon at, the village tax meeting.

Officers, how chosen.

Term of office.

Chief engineer, firemen and engineers; Foremen.

May be paid department.

Expenses, how voted.

Terms of Office—General Regulations.

§ 10. All officers of this corporation shall hold their offices, respectively, unless sooner removed or disqualified, until their successors are chosen and duly qualify.

Village officers to hold until successors are chosen.

Powers of Certain Officers at Fires.

§ 11. The president of said village, the trustees and police constable, the chief engineer and his assistants, and each of them, shall have power to keep away from the vicinity of any fire all idle or suspicious persons, and compel all persons to aid in the extinguishment of fires and the preservation of property exposed to damage thereat; and any person who shall disobey the reason-

Powers of president, trustees, constable and engineers at fires.

Penalty for disobedience. able order of the said officers, or either of them, shall forfeit for the use of the village, twenty-five dollars, to be recovered as other penalties imposed by this act.

President or Board of Trustees have Power to Destroy Buildings.

Recovery of insurance on buildings blown up. § 12. The president or board of trustees shall have power to pull down, blow up and remove buildings for the purpose of arresting the progress of fires and the extinguishment of the same; and in every case where a building shall be pulled down, blown up or removed under the authority of this corporation for the purpose aforesaid, and said building shall be insured, the owner thereof shall be entitled to recover from the said corpo-

Damages to be paid. ration damages for the actual direct injury thus done to any premises, less the amount that any owner, part-owner or lessee of said premises may have received or may be entitled to receive from any insurance company on account of any insurance thereupon. All insurance policies upon said premises or property injured under the provisions of this section, may be assigned to the said "The Board of Trustees of the Village of Geneva," and in such case, and in case there is no insurance upon said building or premises thus injured, then the owner or owners of said premises thus injured shall be entitled to the actual direct damages arising from enforcing the

Rights of village. provisions of this section. The said village of Geneva shall have all rights in and remedies upon any insurance policy assigned under this section, that the original insured or its assignor would have had had no such assignment been made.

Warrants of Appointed Officers.

Warrant or commission. § 13. Every officer appointed by the board of trustees shall receive a proper warrant or commission under the village seal.

TITLE V.

Chap. 294, laws of 1886.

POLICE AND POLICE JUSTICE.

Police Justice.

Term of office. Salary.

§ 1. The police justice shall hold his office four years unless sooner removed. His salary shall be twelve hundred dollars per annum, payable quarterly, and he shall receive or retain no other fee or emolument whatever. He shall, during his term of office, hold no town, county or other village office. He shall have exclusive jurisdiction of all criminal matters within this corporation of which justices of the peace and courts of special sessions now have or shall have jurisdiction within the towns of this State. He shall also have exclusive jurisdiction of all violations of this charter, and all by-laws and ordinances of this village. He shall also have power to take affidavits and acknowledgments subject to the same rules, and in all cases where he could were he a justice of the peace of Ontario county. He shall proceed (without allowing bail to the grand jury) and try all persons brought before him accused of any crime of the grade of misdemeanor or of a less degree, but such person shall have the right of trial by jury, as provided in courts of special sessions, if he shall demand the same. He shall, in all things relating to the mode and manner of procedure in his court, or in the arraignment or trial of parties accused, be governed by the same laws as justices of the peace or courts of special sessions in towns. To enforce the payment of fine imposed by this charter, or the by-laws or ordinances of this village, in addition to other powers, he shall have power to commit the person fined for a number of days certain, not exceeding the number of dollars of the fine, to the Ontario county jail, or any jail or place of confinement that may hereafter be erected in this village, as hereinafter provided, but such commitment shall not exceed twenty days. He shall keep a record of all proceedings before him in which shall be entered all judgments he may render, all fines

To hold no other office.

Jurisdiction.

May take affidavits and acknowledgements.

His powers.

To make out an account against the town.

imposed, and whether collected, and if so, when and how. He shall also make out an account against the town of Geneva, at least yearly, of all criminal matters and proceedings (not including any proceedings to enforce this charter or any by-laws or ordinances of this village) that, before the passage of this act, were proper charges against said town of Geneva, and present the same to the town board or other auditing board or officers of said town, and said town board or other auditing board or officers of said town of Geneva shall audit and allow said account for the same amount as though the same services had been performed by a justice of the peace or court of special sessions of said county. The police justice shall also, at least yearly, make out an account against the county of Ontario for all services that he shall perform, which, before this act, were a county charge against the said county of Ontario, and present the same to the board of supervisors of said county, and said board of supervisors shall audit and allow said account for the same amount as though the services therein charged had been done by a justice of the peace or court of special sessions of said county; and the said board of supervisors of Ontario county shall include in the yearly tax list for said county the amounts thus allowed by the town board, or other auditing board or officer of the town of Geneva, and also the amount allowed by them, and collect the same, and in their warrant attached thereto, direct the collector of the town of Geneva to pay such amounts, when collected, to the treasurer of this village. And said town collector of said town of Geneva shall pay said moneys as thus directed at the same time he pays over other taxes.

Town board to audit same.

Account against county to be made out.

To be audited.

Accounts audited, how to be collected.

Collection of fees and fines.

The police justice shall collect and receive all fees, fines and allowances that are by law collectible by justices of the peace or court of special sessions in towns, or that may be imposed or received by him to enforce this charter or any by-law of this village. And, on or before the tenth day of each month, he shall make and return to the clerk of this village, in such form as the board of trustees may prescribe, a sworn tabular statement of all such fees, fines and allowances

To make monthly reports thereon.

imposed or received by him, either directly or indirectly, during the last month preceding, and with it the receipt of the treasurer of this village, showing that he had paid into the village treasury the amount of all such fees, fines and allowances, as shown by said statement, for the benefit of the village, and any omission to render such statement and pay over such fines, fees and allowances, or any part thereof, on or before the twentieth day of each month, or any false statement, or any intentional omission to set out in such statement any portion of such fines, fees or allowances received by him, shall be sufficient cause for removal of said police justice from office. The board of trustees may also appoint some justice of the peace of the town of Geneva, as hereinbefore provided, and said justice of the peace thus appointed shall, at any time when the police justice shall be unable to perform the duties, or any of them, of his office, on account of necessary absence from this corporation, sickness or any other cause that does not vacate his office, perform all the duties and have all the powers, and be subject to all the regulations herein provided as to said police justice, and for such services he shall receive a proportionate share of the salary of said police justice, to be determined by the board of trustees, which amount paid him shall be deducted from the salary of said police justice. And said justice of the peace shall receive no fees, pay or allowances, from any source, for such services, except such proportionate share of said salary. But said justice of the peace shall make all statements and accounts, as hereinbefore provided, for the period during which he shall discharge the duties of police justice. Said justice of the peace thus designated shall continue to discharge said duties of the police justice during his term of office as said justice of the peace. If both said police justice and said justice of the peace thus designated shall at any time temporarily be absent from this corporation, or unable to perform the duties of this office, the board of trustees may designate any other justice of the peace of the town of Geneva to perform the duties of said office during said temporary absence or inability, and

Penalty.

Trustees may appoint town justice to act in absence of police justice.

Compensation to be deducted from salary of police justice.

Duties and powers of justice thus appointed.

Additional substitute.

provide for payment thereof, and such justice thus designated shall have all the powers of, and be subject to all rules and regulations concerning said police justice, for the time he shall act. But no justice of the peace of the town of Geneva shall receive any fees, emoluments or pay from any source, for the performance of any duties, or the issuing of any process of which the police justice by this act, has jurisdiction, except as provided in this act

No other justice to receive fees.

Chap. 623, laws of 1874.

The police justice shall have concurrent jurisdiction with justices of the peace of all criminal matters within the town of Geneva of which the justices of the peace and courts of special sessions thereof now have or shall have jurisdiction within the towns of this State.

Police justice, concurrent jurisdiction.

Police Constable and Extra Police.

Powers and duties of police constable.

§ 2. The police constable shall possess the same powers, rights and privileges, and be subject to the same duties and liabilities, as appertain and belong to the constables in the several towns of this state. He shall also perform all such services as the by-laws of this corporation may require. It shall be his special duty to see that all by-laws of this village are enforced; but any constable of the town of Geneva shall have the same powers to serve all process to enforce said by-laws as the police constable. For the purpose of arrest within this corporation of all offenders against the laws of this state or by-laws of this corporation, and of taking and detaining said offender until he can be brought before the police justice or justice of the peace performing his duties, all extra police or night watchmen shall have all the powers of and rights, and be subject to all the liabilities of, the police constable.

Other constables.

Extra police and night watchmen, powers of.

Chap. 623, laws of 1874.

The said police constable and said extra police or night watchmen shall have power and authority respectively

NOTE—Chap. 623, June 9, 1874.—§ 9. The said act is hereby amended by striking out the words "town of Seneca," wherever the same occur in said act, or in any amendments thereof, and inserting instead thereof the words "town of Geneva."

to arrest any person or persons by them found violating any of the penal ordinances or by-laws of this corporation, and to take such person or persons before the police justice, to be dealt with the same as if such person or persons had been arrested upon warrant or civil process theretofore duly issued by such justice.

Summary arrests for violation of ordinances.

Ex-officio Police Constable.

§ 3. Each member of the board of trustees shall be, ex-officio, police constable, and when acting as such shall have the same powers as are in this act conferred upon the extra police.

Trustees ex-officio police constables.

Fees of Officers Executing Process.

§ 4. For any services in behalf of, or within this corporation, or under this charter, the police constable, any town constable or other officer, or any person deputized to act as such, shall only charge and receive fees but for one warrant for the arrest of any one person, however many warrants he may then have, and on but one subpœna for subpœnaing any one person to attend any court or examination, however many subpœnas he may have at one time, and only one travel fee for the distance actually traveled by said police constable, officer or person deputized to act as such, in the actual performance of his duty as an officer, for any one person as aforesaid; but in case of the arrest of more than one person at one time, the officer making such arrest may be allowed such further amount as shall be just, to pay him for such additional expenses as shall be necessarily caused by such arrest of more than one person.

Fees of officers executing process.

TITLE VI.

OF THE TAX MEETING, AND THE ASSESSMENT AND COLLECTION OF TAXES.

Tax Meeting.

Chap. 294, laws of 1886.

Annual tax meeting, when to be held.

§ 1. The annual tax meeting of the tax payers of the village of Geneva shall be held on the third Tuesday of May, commencing at ten o'clock A. M. At least two weeks before said meeting the board of trustees shall carefully examine into and determine the amount of money that will be needed for properly carrying out the provisions of this charter, and to carry on the village government for the next year, and shall make a tabular statement of such amount, and of the separate purpose and object for which such expenditure is calculated to be made, stating such object or purpose and the amount needed therefor. They shall also carefully examine the streets of said village, and shall determine and fix upon an aggregate amount that in their judgment will be needed to keep said streets in good repair for the next year. The board of trustees shall also prepare a statement of the money on hand at the commencement of the previous year (as stated in the account of the year previous to that as cash on hand), of all moneys received by them under any by-law, or in any way in or by virtue of their official capacity, and the sources from which received, of all moneys expended by them and the objects for which expended, and showing the balance on hand on the last day of April previous to such tax meeting. Said last statement of receipts and expenditures shall be signed by a majority of the board of trustees, and verified under an oath or affirmation by the clerk and treasurer to be correct. They shall publish both such statements in the village papers at least one week before said meeting, and shall, in connection therewith, and at the same time, state the place where, within said corporation, said annual tax meeting shall be held. Said tax meeting shall elect a committee of three citizens to ex-

Trustees to submit estimate and statement of money requisite.

Examination of streets.

Annual financial statement to be made.

To be signed, verified and published.

amine the above sworn accounts of the receipts and expenditures when made out, and the vouchers therefor, and said committee shall report thereupon to the tax meeting to which said accounts are presented, before any other business after organization. At each annual tax meeting after the passage of this act, the said tax meeting shall elect a committee of three citizens to examine such accounts for the next ensuing year, and said committee shall, within one week before the tax meeting to which they are to report and before the said tax meeting, examine the above accounts and the vouchers therefor, and said committee shall be prepared to report thereon, and shall report thereon as early as may be after organization. It shall be the duty of the board of trustees and all officers to allow said committee to examine any and all books and vouchers of this corporation. The aggregate amount reported for street expenses shall be voted on as a whole Its amount may be decreased by a vote of the meeting, but cannot be increased, and said sum thus voted shall be applied in repair of the streets under the direction of the board of trustees. The meeting may also vote a tax for any of the objects specified in said report of the board of trustees, published, and shall vote upon all expenditures proposed by the board of trustees. After all the proposed expenditures of the trustees as published, are voted upon, then the tax meeting may vote upon any other proposed expenditure for any particular object proposed, provided notice of said proposed expenditure be given in the village papers, as herein required of the board of trustees. The trustees are empowered and authorized to raise money by tax to pay all contingent and stated expenses of this corporation, and also to carry into effect the several powers and privileges granted by this act; but no tax (except for the salaries of officers fixed by this act, or by by-laws) shall be levied or collected, until or unless the same shall have been authorized by a vote of the taxable inhabitants, at the annual tax meeting, or at a special tax meeting of the taxable inhabitants called for the purpose of authorizing the assessment and collection of taxes; and the said

Powers of committee. Books and vouchers.

Street expenses, how voted on.

Other objects to be voted on.

Tax not proposed by trustees may be voted upon notice.

Trustees empowered to levy tax.

contingent and stated expenses shall be presented to such tax meeting in items specifically, and shall be voted on item by item; and no contingent expenses not thus voted upon shall be collected, and no part of money voted for any one purpose can be used for any other; and if not used as voted, shall remain as part of the unexpended balance in the treasury and reported as such; except, however, that a sum, not to exceed one thousand dollars in any one year, may be raised in bulk, to pay unforeseen and necessary expenses, to be known as "special contingent" fund, and to be advertised, voted and expended in the same manner as other items. But the amount of taxes to be raised in any one year over and above street expenses, salaries fixed by this charter or by by-laws, shall not exceed one *per cent. of the assessed valuation of the said village for the year eighteen hundred and seventy-two. Any balance in the treasury of this village, not expended for the purpose voted, may be disposed of and applied to other purposes by a vote of the annual tax meeting.

Money not to be diverted.

Aggregate tax limited.

Balances how disposed of.

Qualifications of Voters.

Voters at tax meeting.

§ 2. No person shall be qualified or permitted to vote upon any tax for street expenses, or upon any other tax or appropriation, who shall not appear, upon the last annual assessment roll, to have been assessed and taxed for real or personal property; and all votes for taxes and appropriations of any kind, or for any purpose, shall be taken and determined as provided in section three hereof; and all public meetings for voting taxes or appropriations shall be called for and commence at ten o'clock in the forenoon.

When tax meetings to commence.

Mode of Voting.

Mode of voting.

§ 3. The votes upon any tax or appropriation of money shall be taken by each legal voter passing between two

* NOTE.—The assessment roll of 1872 footed up $2,086,322.72.

tellers, who shall, at each meeting, be appointed from among the legal voters present by the presiding officer of the meeting; and such tellers shall, as soon as all the votes on any question are taken, report the result to the meeting.

Mode of Assessment.

§ 4. Whenever any tax shall have been voted to be raised, as herein provided, the assessors shall apportion the same among the taxable inhabitants of the corporation and non-resident owners of property therein, and corporate bodies therein, in just proportions according to the last assessment roll, or according to a new one when thereunto required; and a new assessment roll shall be made at least once in each year. They shall assess every male inhabitant, of lawful age, of the corporation the sum of one dollar, as poll tax, to be levied and collected as other taxes, in addition to any other tax assessed to him; and they may add to the tax to be assessed, against each individual who shall have refused or neglected to pay his tax of any former year, the amount of his tax so unpaid; they shall give ten days' notice of the time and place at which they will meet to review the assessment roll, which shall be given by notices posted in five of the most public places in the corporation. When the assessors' roll shall have been reviewed and completed, the assessors shall deliver the same to the president, with their certificates annexed thereto, signed by a majority of them. The trustees shall annex to such list their warrant, signed by a majority of them, and then deliver the same to the collector, who shall thereupon proceed to collect the several sums specified therein, in the manner herein directed, and shall pay such moneys into the treasury within such time as shall be prescribed in said warrant, which warrant may be renewed from time to time, and as often and for such length of time at each renewal as the trustees shall deem meet, and the collector shall, by virtue of any such renewal, have all the powers and

Assessors to apportion tax.

Poll tax.

Re-assessment authorized

Review of assessment.

Complete roll to be delivered to president.

Warrant to collector.

Renewal of warrant.

authority and rights which are obtained by the original warrant.

Chap. 623, laws of 1874. Re-taxation, property how described.

Upon any re-taxation or re-assessment, in cases where any individual shall have refused or neglected to pay his tax of any former year, as above provided, the property re-taxed or re-assessed shall be definitely described in the assessment roll.

Special Meeting—How Called.

Special village meetings.

§ 5. The trustees are authorized to call meetings of the electors whenever they deem such meetings necessary for any purpose; and it shall be their duty to call such meetings at any time when they shall be requested in writing to do so by any six inhabitants of the corporation who shall be liable to pay taxes; and the trustees shall give notice of such meetings in like manner as is directed for the annual election of officers of thê corporation. The notice of every special meeting of the taxpayers of this village shall specify the objects for which it is called, and nothing can be done thereat unless thus specified in said notice.

How called.

For specified objects.

Mode Collecting Taxes.

Collector's notice.

§ 6. Whenever the collector shall have received any warrant and tax list for the collection of taxes, he shall immediately thereafter cause notices of the reception thereof to be posted up in five public places in the said village, and so located as will be most likely to give notice to the inhabitants thereof and shall publish such notice in all the village papers, and shall designate in such notices a central and convenient place in said village, where he will attend from nine o'clock in the forenoon till three o'clock in the afternoon of each day, at least fifteen days, exclusive of Sundays, for the purpose of receiving payment of taxes; and it shall be the duty of such collector to attend accordingly; and any person may pay his taxes to such collector at the time and place so designated, or at any other time or place, on paying one per

Payment of taxes.

cent. fees thereon, within fifteen days, exclusive of Sundays, from the first posting of said notices: and no collector shall receive more than one per cent. for receiving or collecting any taxes within said fifteen days; but every such collector shall be entitled to receive one cent fees on every fractional amount of tax under one dollar, paid in or collected within said fifteen days. It shall be the duty of the collector, after the expiration of said fifteen days, to proceed and collect unpaid taxes in the same manner as is provided by law for the collection of taxes by town collectors, and shall pay over or account to the village treasurer; and he shall have all the powers and rights to enforce collection thereof given by law to town collectors; and he shall be entitled to charge, collect and receive on such unpaid taxes, the fees which shall be voted or allowed to him by the provisions of this act; which said fees shall be collected with such unpaid taxes from the several respective persons named in said tax list. Whenever the assessors shall make out any tax list and warrant, they shall not add thereto the fees for the collection; but such fees shall be paid and collected as above described and set forth.

Collector's fees.

Collection of unpaid taxes.

Powers and rights of collector.

Neglect or Refusal to Pay.

§ 7. Whenever any person or corporation, upon whose real estate a tax or assessment shall be imposed or assessed in pursuance of this act, shall refuse or neglect to pay the same within the life of the warrant issued for the collection thereof, and there shall be no sufficient personal property of such person or corporation found within the limits of said village whereof the same can be levied and collected, the collector holding such warrant shall make return thereof, under oath, subscribed by him, to the trustees, who are thereupon hereby authorized to cause the real estate on which such tax or assessment was imposed or assessed to be sold at public auction for a term of time for the payment of such tax or assessment, giving six weeks' notice of such sale in a newspaper published in the village

Sale of real estate for non-payment of tax.

Notice of sale how published.

of Geneva, and serving personal notice on the owner of such real estate, if he be a resident of said village, and if not a resident, then serving notice by mail on such owner, if his place of residence be known to said trustees and also by giving the like notice to the occupant of the premises if occupied by a tenant; and the said real estate shall be sold to the person who will offer to take the same for the shortest term for the payment of such tax and assessment, with interest thereon from the date of the warrant, and the fees of the publication of such notice. But the owner, his agent or assigns, may, within one year after such sale, redeem the same, by paying or tendering the purchaser, or his legal representative, or to the treasurer of the village, the amount of the bid at such sale, with interest at the rate of fourteen per cent. per annum, and all the provisions of the act entitled "An act authorizing mortgages to redeem real estate sold for taxes and assessments," passed May fourteenth, eighteen hundred and forty, shall apply to any such sale; and any mortgagee of such premises, or any part thereof, shall have the benefit of said act; and the notice required to be given by the second section of said act shall not be given until after the time limited for the owner or his assigns to redeem.

Manner of sale.

Right of redemption.

Rights of mortgagees.

Sale of Land.

Purchaser of real estate on tax sale entitled to certificate.

§ 8. When any real estate shall be sold for the collection of any tax or assessment, and the owner thereof, his agents, heirs or assigns, shall not, within one year thereafter, have paid or tendered to the purchaser thereof, or his legal representatives, or to the treasurer of the village, the amount of the bid on such sale, and the same shall not have been redeemed by any mortgage of such real estate within three months after the expiration of one year, as above provided, with interest at the rate of fourteen per cent. per annum from and after the time of such sale, the trustees shall deliver to the purchaser, or his assigns, a certificate of such sale, under the seal of the village, and signed by the president and clerk, the execution whereof may be proved and acknowledged in

How executed.

the same manner as a deed, and which may in like manner and with like effect be recorded as other conveyances of real estate.

Title of Purchaser at Sale.

§ 9. The purchaser at any such sale on receiving such certificate, or his executor, administrator or assigns, may immediately enter into possession of such real estate, and hold, occupy and enjoy during the time for which it was sold as aforesaid, and such certificate shall in all courts and places, be held presumptive evidence of the right of such purchaser, his heirs or assigns, to the possession of such premises during the time, as against the owners, or those claiming under them; and all the buildings put on the premises during such term by the purchaser, his heirs or assigns, may be removed at or before the expiration thereof. If any person having or claiming possession, shall, on demand of the purchaser or holder of such certificate, refuse to yield possession of said premises thus sold, or any portion thereof, such purchaser or holder of said certificate shall be entitled to the same remedy to recover such possession as is by law provided for the removal of tenants holding over after the expiration of their terms.

Purchaser when to enter into possession.

Removal of buildings.

Remedy of purchaser to recover possession.

Entry of Sale by Clerk.

§ 10. It shall be the duty of the clerk, in all cases of such sale, to make one entry of the same in the minutes of said board, with a description of the property sold, the amount for which the same was sold, the length of term or time, and the name of the purchaser, and the time of and the amount paid for the redemption in case the same shall be redeemed.

Entry of sale by clerk.

Other Remedies.

§ 11. In addition to the modes of collection of taxes herein provided, the board of trustees or the collector may bring an action for any tax, in the name of this cor-

Taxes may be collected by action at law.

poration, against the persons assessed, or the owner of the land taxed, in any court of this state having civil jurisdiction, and in case of judgment being rendered for any such tax, or any portion thereof, double the ordinary costs shall be allowed by said court and included in any judgment rendered; and in case in any such action it shall be alleged and proven that such person, thus prosecuted, has wilfully refused to pay such tax without sufficient cause, and being able to pay the same, then, but not otherwise, a body execution may issue for the collection of any judgment rendered in such case, as in cases for torts. And in such cases the board of trustees may prosecute for such tax before the police justice provided for by this act, and in case it is proven that such tax or any portion of it is unpaid, and that such person against whom said tax had been assessed, and who is thus proceeded against, has wilfully refused to pay such tax under the circumstances above stated, then the said police justice may proceed to collect such tax, or any portion thereof unpaid, with double costs as above provided, as a fine or penalty imposed by this act, and in such cases all remedies in this act provided for the collection of fines or the imposition of penalties, may be used to collect such tax and costs; but no body execution shall be issued against any female, nor shall any female be proceeded against before the police justice, as in this section provided. All the modes provided by the charter for the collection of taxes and assessments are hereby declared to be concurrent remedies, but only one can be used at one time, although each may be used in succession. One may be discontinued and another adopted at any time, but only one bill of costs shall be collected from the tax payer. All such judgments, and all moneys received by the board of trustees or collector in the collection of unpaid taxes, shall be immediately paid into the village treasury, and shall belong to said village.

Proceedings thereon.

Costs recoverable.

Body execution.

Jurisdiction of police justice.

Collections from females

Concurrent remedies.

Judgments to be paid into village treasury.

Expenditures for Extraordinary Purposes.

§ 12. Whenever the board of trustees shall be of the opinion that the interest of said village requires the expenditure for any extraordinary or special purpose, which, in their opinion, cannot be paid from the said sums to be voted by the tax meeting, as hereinbefore mentioned, after defraying the ordinary current expenses of the year, the said board of trustees shall have the power to call a special election; but before ordering such election they shall make an estimate of the sum necessary to be raised for said purposes, and shall state the amount and the objects for which it is required, together with the reasons for their opinions, and cause the statement to be published in one or more village papers, two weeks successively, preceding the day of such election. The board of trustees may, after making and publishing such statement, give two weeks' notice of an election, and shall designate in said notice some convenient place in said village for holding the polls of said election, and the time when it shall be held. The trustees shall be inspectors of the poll of said election, in the same manner as at charter elections in said village. Every executor, administrator, devisee, heir, guardian or agent named in the assessment roll made by the assessors of said village next preceding said special election, as the possessor or representative of property assessed therein shall, if he is a resident and twenty-one years of age, be considered as a qualified voter at said election. The said assessment roll made by the assessors, or a copy thereof certified by the village clerk and the president of said village, shall be evidence of the names and assessments, as aforesaid. The polls of said election shall be opened and closed in the manner provided for holding charter elections in said village. On the ballots deposited on said special election shall be written or printed, or partly written and partly printed, on the inside thereof, "for special tax" or "against special tax." The votes received at such special election shall be canvassed, and the result certified, and the certificates thereof filed as provided by the fourth sec-

Trustees may call special election to vote extraordinary tax.

To submit and publish estimate.

Notice of election, how given.

Inspectors of election.

Rights of executors, heirs, guardians, &c., to vote.

Assessment roll to be evidence.

Polls, time of opening and closing.

Form of ballots

Canvass and certificate of result.

tion of title two of this act; and the board of trustees at their next meeting after said election shall cause the result as appearing by said certificate to be entered in their minutes, and if it shall appear that the whole number of votes received at such election, with the words "for special tax," shall exceed the whole number of votes "against special tax," it shall be the duty of the board of trustees to cause the said sum of money so voted for to be assessed, levied and raised with and in addition to all other taxes in and by the next assessment roll, or in and by not more than three successive annual installments thereafter, and in the same manner and with the same force and authority as herein described, conferred in reference to other village taxes; provided, always, that the total amount proposed to be raised in any one year, as voted for at special election or elections, shall not exceed ten thousand dollars. In case of a majority of votes "for special tax," the board of trustees may thereupon proceed to authorize the expenditure of the amount thereof, and may borrow, if they shall deem it necessary to do so, the amount so voted in anticipation of the collection of said tax, for a time not exceeding three years, payable in equal annual installments, if loan shall be made for more than one year, which installments shall be levied and collected in the same manner as the general tax of the village; and the amount so borrowed shall be expended upon the objects for which the special tax is raised, and shall be paid as soon as the same becomes due from the avails of the tax. The sum and sums of money raised by any special tax shall be paid to and kept by the treasurer distinct from other money, and entered into a separate account, and shall be appropriated by the board of trustees exclusively to the object or objects mentioned in their said published statement.

Trustees to levy tax.

May be raised in installments.

Limitation of special tax.

Trustees to make expenditures.

Power to borrow money.

Treasurer to keep account of special tax money.

TITLE VII.

OF STREETS, HIGHWAYS AND PUBLIC IMPROVEMENTS.

Board of Trustees to be Commissioners of Highways.

SECTION 1. The trustees shall be commissioners of highways, and are vested with and authorized to exercise and perform, within the bounds of the corporation, the same rights, powers and duties as are possessed and exercised by the commissioners of highways in the several towns; *except that they shall not be liable, as such highway commissioners, neither shall the village of Geneva be liable for any damage or injury arising from an accumulation of ice or snow upon any of the sidewalks or public places within the corporate limits of said village, unless written notice shall have been served upon the board of trustees, or upon the village clerk at least twenty-four hours before the happening of such damage or injury, which said notice shall be signed by the complainant, and shall particularly set forth and describe the place complained of.* Said trustees are also authorized and empowered to lay out, alter and open or discontinue any street in any part of the corporation, of such width and in such place as they shall deem necessary and proper, and may provide for and direct the raising, grading, leveling, paving, repairing, mending, planking, macadamizing and cleaning any street in the corporation, subject to the provisions of this act, and as therein prescribed. But no street shall be laid out or altered, except upon the petition of twelve freeholders of the corporation, none of whom shall be in any way interested in the lands proposed to be taken for such street. The territory contained within the bounds of said village shall be exempt from the supervision of commissioners of highways of the town of Geneva. The trustees may lay out any street through any lands, building, garden, orchard or inclosure in said village.

Chap. 241, laws of 1888.

Trustees to have powers of commissioners of highways.

Not liable for accidents unless upon written notice of dangerous place.

Petition of 12 freeholders required.

Village exempt from supervision of commissioners of town.

Powers of trustees in laying out streets.

§ 2. Whenever any street, alley, lane or public ground is laid out, altered, widened or straightened, by virtue of

Chap. 411, laws of 1889.

this act, or any local improvement is made under and by virtue of this act, which requires that private property shall be taken for public purposes, the board of trustees shall in the first instance, and before making such improve-

Proceedings to take lands for streets, etc.

ment, give notice of their intention to take and appropriate the land necessary therefor and to make such improvement, by publishing such notice, specifying, as near as may be, the lands to be taken, in one or more of the village papers, which notice, shall also notify the owners of such lands, that, at any time within three weeks from the

Notice to be given by publication.

date of said notice they may file with the clerk of said village their claim or claims for damage by reason of such improvement, and that application will be made to the county court of Ontario county, or, in case it is not in session then to the county judge of said county, for the appointment of three commissioners residing in said vil-

Application for appointment of commissioners.

lage, to ascertain the damages so claimed, and to assess the expense of such improvement, or so much thereof as may be proper, upon the lands and premises to be benefited thereby; which notice shall also specify the improvement to be made,

Commissioners to be appointed.

the time when and place where such application will be made. At the time and place so specified the board of trustees, by such person as they shall designate, shall make application to the said court or judge for the appointment of such commissioners, and said claimants shall have the right to to be heard thereon. The said court or county judge shall thereupon, by a rule to be entered in the clerk's office of Ontario county, appoint said three commissioners to ascertain and assess the damage so claimed, and at the same

Their powers and duties.

time to determine what persons will be benefited by such improvement, and to assess the damages and expenses thereof, or such portion thereof as they shall deem just, upon the persons so benefited, in proportion, as near as may be, to the benefit resulting to each. The hearing of

Commissioners to take oath.

such application may be adjourned from time to time by such court or judge. The commissioners shall be sworn by any person authorized to administer oaths, faithfully

To view premises and receive evidence.

and impartially to execute their duty in making such assessments according to their ability; they shall view the premises, receive any legal evidence, and may adjourn from day to day. They shall, before entering upon their duties, give notice to said claimants of the time and place of their meeting, at least five days before the time of such meeting, by publishing such notice in one or more of the village papers. They shall determine and award to the owner or owners of such land so claiming damages such damages as they will, in their opinion, sustain by the completion of the improvements, after making due allowance for any benefit which said owner or owners may derive therefrom. They shall, at the same time, assess and apportion the said damages and expenses of such improvement, or such portion thereof as they shall deem just, on the real estate benefited thereby, as nearly as may be in proportion to the benefits resulting therefrom, and shall briefly describe the real estate on which any assessment is made by them. If there be any buildings on the land taken for such improvement, the value of such buildings to remove shall be ascertained in their assessment, and the owner thereof may remove the same in ten days, or in such other time as the board of trustees shall allow after the confirmation of the return of the commissioners. If he shall so remove said building, the value thereof so ascertained shall be deducted from the damages awarded to him. The determination and assessment of the commissioners, signed by them, shall be returned by them to the trustees within thirty days of their appointment. The said court or judge may, if sufficient objections are made to the appointment of said commissioners, or if any of said commissioners shall refuse or be unable to serve, appoint others in their places, in the manner above provided, and the board of trustees, after the determination and assessment of the commissioners is returned to them, shall give two weeks' notice in one or more of the village papers, that the same will on a day specified in said notice, be confirmed, unless objections, by some person or persons interested, are made thereto in writing and filed with the clerk. If no such objections are made as aforesaid, the determination and assessment shall be confirmed by the board of trustees. If objections are so made, any person interested may be

Notice to claimants.

The award and determination.

Assessment of damages and expenses.

Removal of buildings.

Determination to be returned to trustees.

Court may appoint other commissioners.

Notice of hearing objections to confirmation by trustees.

Trustees to confirm or refer back assessment.

heard before the board of trustees touching the matter, on the day specified in said notice, or on such other days as the board of trustees shall appoint. The said board of trustees shall either confirm such determination and assessment, or annul the same and refer the same matter back to the same commissioners, or other commissioners to be appointed by such court for the like purpose. The commissioners shall proceed in all things in making and returning the second assessment as in making and returning the first assessment, and the said trustees shall proceed thereon as though it were an orginal assessment. In case the board of trustees shall confirm either assessment and determination, the same shall be final and conclusive on all persons interested, except as herein provided, but in case the board of trustees shall annul both, then all proceedings in relation thereto shall be null and void; but nothing herein contained shall authorize the board to discontinue or contract any street or highway, or any part thereof, without the consent in writing of two-thirds of all persons owning lands adjoining thereon. On final confirmation of the report and assessment the same, together with a copy thereof, shall be filed with the village clerk and in the clerk's office of Ontario county. Before any local improvement is made as above provided, the board of trustees shall cause notice of the same to be published in one or more of the village papers for at least three weeks. Objections to confirming the determination and assessment of the commissioners as above provided may be made also by any tax payer of said corporation or village, in the same manner as person or persons immediately interested. Whenever in the opinion of the board of trustees, and the village board of health, it is deemed necessary that a public sewer be constructed in any portion of the village which from the nature of the ground, or other cause, will need to be carried in whole or in part, through private lands, the said board of trustees may order such sewer made, by a resolution to be entered on its minutes, and may at once proceed to have the necessary lands condemned in the same manner as hereinbefore provided for laying out, altering or widening any

Proceedings when referred back.

Second assessment when confirmed to be final.

Annulling proviso.

Streets may not be discontinued or contracted without consent of two-thirds of owners.

Local improvements, notice of.

Objections to assessment of commissioners.

Sewers, construct, manner of proceeding; how to pay for.

street, alley or lane, or making any other public improvement, the damages and benefits to be assessed and paid for, and all other proceedings had in like manner and in the same force and effect as hereinbefore provided in this section for the taking of private lands for public purposes. Such taking however shall be construed to mean the necessary use only of the lands in question for the construction and proper maintenance of the sewer and its several connections. In determining the damages and benefit hereunder the commissioners shall consider all lands affected by the proposed sewer, whether such lands are immediately contiguous to the line of the sewer or not, and such lands shall be made to bear their just proportion of the damages and benefits in like manner and as fully as if the sewer passed directly through them. Before any proceedings however are had hereunder, in the way of constructing a public sewer or having the lands condemned, the board of trustees shall have a survey made by a competent engineer laying out the line of said sewer, and, as far as may be, an estimate made of the cost, the expenses of which survey and estimate shall be deemed part of the cost of the sewer, and shall be added to the other expenses; and, for the purposes of making said survey and estimate, the board, by its duly authorized agents may enter upon any and all lands necessary, and shall be liable only for any actual damage done to the lands or property of the owners or occupants. Any portion of the cost and expense of the sewer or any of its branches, including cost of survey or the expenses of the commission, which in the judgment of the commissioners, is properly chargeable to the village of Geneva at large, shall, upon the report of the commissioners being confirmed, be paid by the board of trustees out of any unappropriated moneys in the hands of the village treasurer.

Real Estate Subject to Lease.

§ 3. In all cases where the whole or any part of any real estate, subject to any lease or other agreement, shall be

Proceedings in case lands taken are subject to lease.

taken by the board of trustees under this title, all the covenants and stipulations contained in such lease or agreement shall, upon final confirmation of the assessment thereof, cease, determine and be absolutely discharged; and in all cases where a part only of any real estate shall be so taken, the said covenants and stipulations shall be so discharged only as to the part so taken; the Ontario county judge may, on application in writing of either or any party in interest to such lease or agreement, appoint three disinterested freeholders of the village, resident therein, to determine the rents, payments, and conditions which shall thereafter be paid and performed, under such lease or agreement, in respect to the residue of such real estate; and the report of such freeholders, or any two of them, under their hands, on being confirmed by the judge, shall be binding and conclusive on all persons interested in such real estate.

Three disinterested freeholders to be appointed and their determination when confirmed to be final.

Appeal to County Court.

Notice of confirmation to be given.

§ 4. If any such assessment or determination of the commissioners be confirmed, the trustees shall forthwith give notice of such confirmation to all persons who shall have filed objections thereto by personal service upon such objectors as can be found within said village, and by mail upon all others. Within ten days after the service of such notice, or at any time within fifteen days from the confirmation of said assessment, any person who shall have filed objections as aforesaid, or any other person considering himself aggrieved by such determination or assessment, may appeal from the same and from the confirmation thereof to the county court of Ontario county, anything hereinbefore to the contrary notwithstanding, by filing with the clerk of said village, and serving on each of said commissioners personally, or by leaving the same at his usual place of residence, a notice of such appeal, stating the grounds thereof. Said appeal shall operate as a stay of all proceedings under said assessment until the hearing and decision thereof, and no private property shall be taken

Appeals to county clerk.

Mode of appealing.

Stay of proceedings.

or improvement commenced under the provisions of this title until after the expiration of the time herein limited for appealing. The said commissioners, or a majority of them, shall, within ten days after such service on them, return to the county court of Ontario county, and file with the clerk thereof, a full return of all evidence taken and proceedings had before them, and the reasons for their decisions. The said village clerk shall also, in like manner and within the same time, return the report of said commissioners and all proceedings had thereon by the board of trustees. Such commissioners and clerk may be compelled to make or amend their respective returns in the same manner as justices of the peace, on appeal from their judgments. Said appeal may be brought on for trial by either party, at any time, before said county court, on notice of ten days, and shall be heard and determined by said court without a jury, upon the said determination and assessment, the returns of said commissioners and said clerk, and the notice of appeal. But said court may, in case any party to such appeal show that he could not, by due diligence, have procured the attendance of any witnesses or the production of any legal testimony before said commissioners, but not otherwise, on the hearing of said appeal, examine such further witnesses and receive such further evidence as any party may thus show he could not have procured, as may be produced by either party, and in such case any party to said appeal may answer such evidence thus admitted. Such court may set aside, affirm or modify such assessment and determination in such manner as it may deem proper, and the determination of said court thereupon shall be final. Said county court shall at all times be open to hear all matters of which it has jurisdiction by this act. The said commissioners shall each be entitled to receive two dollars per day while actually engaged in all proceedings by or before them; said per diem allowance for all proceedings by and before them prior to said appeal shall be paid by the said village, and such per diem allowance for all proceedings by or before them subsequent to said appeal shall be paid by said appellant

Commissioners to make return.

Clerk to make return.

Return. How compelled.

Appeals when tried.

Further evidence to be taken.

Court may affirm, modify or set aside assessment.

Pay of commissioners.

or said village, as said county court shall order and direct.

Expenses and damages for taking private property, how assessed.

§ 5. All expenses and damages for taking private property in opening streets, or making any other public improvement, as assessed and determined by this charter, or as agreed upon by the owners with the board of trustees, excepting and deducting therefrom such portion of such expenses and damages as shall be assessed upon and collected from the property adjoining or from the owners ~~thereof, shall be collected by tax as any other expense.~~ But before any tax shall be levied for such purpose it must be authorized by a vote of the village tax meeting.

County court to determine whether requirements have been carried out.

§ 6. On any appeal from the assessment and determination of said commissioners and the confirmation thereof, the county court shall also have jurisdiction to examine and determine, in such manner as said court may order, whether or not all the provisions and requirements of this act for opening any street, or making any improvement which shall require taking private property, have been fully and fairly carried out and fulfilled by the board of trustees or other officer of this village, or other person, and on such hearing may set aside any such proceeding, or order such further proceedings to be taken to perfect the same, as to such court may seem just and proper, and, unless such proceedings thus ordered are taken as prescribed, such proceedings shall be void.

May set aside and order further proceedings.

Damages to be Tendered Owners.

Trustees to pay or tender amount of awards.

§ 7. When the amount of any damages for taking lands as aforesaid shall be ascertained by a final confirmation of the report and assessment of the commissioners, the board of trustees shall, within one year thereafter, pay or tender the amount of such damages to the owners of lands and tenements to whom the same shall have been allowed ; and in case such owners shall refuse the same, or be unknown, non-residents of the village, married women, infants, lunatics, or the rights and interests of the persons claiming the same shall, in the opinion of the board of trustees, be doubtful, it shall in such case be lawful for the board of trustees to pay the amount of damages into the office of the clerk of the county court of the county of Ontario, accompanied by a statement of the facts and circumstances under which such payment is made, and describing the lands and tenements taken by the village for which such damages have been awarded. The damages so paid into the county court shall be invested and paid over by it in the same manner that other moneys are paid over by said court. Until such damages shall be so paid, it shall not be lawful for the board of trustees to take or enter upon such lands or tenements, for the taking of which any such damages shall be allowed.

To deposit awards for unknown owners, infants, &c.

Until paid lands not to be taken

Assessment to be a Lien on Lands.

§ 8. Whenever any proceedings shall have been had under sections one or two or this title, and the commissioners appointed as therein specified shall have made their estimate and assessment, and the same shall have been confirmed by the board of trustees, if it shall then appear from such report that assessments for benefit are made against owners of property therein, such assessments, from the date of the confirmation of said report, shall be a lien on the lands in respect to which such assessment had been made, having preference over all other liens and incumbrances whatever, and such assessments shall be collected in all respects as provided in the sixth title of this act for the collection of the assessments therein specified.

Assessments to be a lien on lands.

Chap. 411, laws of 1889.

How collected.

Expenses of Improving Streets—How Paid.

§ 9. All expenses of working, paving, repairing, improving and cleaning the streets shall be denominated street expenses, and shall be paid by a tax on the whole village, voted as herein provided, except in case of paving or making sewers therein, where the board of trustees shall assess a portion of the cost of the same upon the owners of the property adjoining, and in such cases all expenses

All street expenses to be paid by tax.

Exception.

other than that portion thus assessed on the owners of the adjoining property, shall be included and paid as street expenses.

Expenses—When a Portion may be Assessed on Owners of Adjoining Lands.

Assessments for street improvements upon property benefitted.

Sprinkling streets

Chap. 241, laws of 1888.

§ 10. Whenever it is proposed to improve any street, or portion thereof, by paving the same with stone, iron, wood or other hard substance, or by building any public sewer through the same, *or for the public health or convenience, to cause the same to be sprinkled with water*, the board or trustees shall have power to determine, by a resolution to be entered in the minutes of its proceedings, what part or portion, if any, of the expenses of any such improvement shall be assessed on any real estate or lot adjacent, which they shall deem will be particularly benefited by such expenditure and improvement. If they shall make any determination in relation to particular benefits, they shall make a certificate thereof and file the same with the clerk, who shall enter the same in the minutes of the proceedings of the board; such certificate shall specify what real estate or lot is so benefited, the name of the occupant or owner thereof, if known, the amount of such benefit, and a brief description of the real estate or lot on which the amount of such benefit is chargeable, which amount shall be a lien thereon, and may be recovered by the village in an action brought therefor against the owner or any occupant of said real estate or lot, together with costs and interest from the date of filing such certificate. If the said amount of benefit shall not be paid or the owner of said real estate or lot shall be a non-resident, the trustees shall proceed to sell the same and collect said amount thereby, together with the interest, cost and charges of sale, in the manner directed by title six of this act, to collect a tax by sale of real estate; but the board of trustees shall not thus assess any portion of said expenditure as provided in this section upon the lands to be particularly benefited, unless the owners of said lands or lots of at least two-thirds in value

Determination thereof, how filled.

Lien, how recovered.

Lands may be sold for unpaid assessments.

Consent of two-thirds of land owners requisite to make assessment.

thus proposed to be assessed, or persons who are willing and liable to pay at least two-thirds of such assessment, shall consent in writing to the same, which consent, thus signed, shall be filed and entered on the records of this village before any such assessment shall be fully made.

Sidewalks—How Made, Repaired, Cleaned and Paid For.

§ 11. The trustees of said village shall have power to cause the sidewalks on the streets and highways within the said village, or any or either of them, or any part thereof, to be graded, leveled, raised, amended, graveled, stoned, paved, flagged, curbed, planked and repaired, and to compel the owners or occupants of any lands or lots adjoining such streets or highways to make such improvements upon the sidewalks as foresaid, in front of or adjoining said land or lots, and to determine and prescribe the manner of doing the same, and the materials to be used therein, and the quality of such materials; and, for the purpose of carrying into effect the foregoing provisions of this section, the said trustees shall cause to be served an order or notice, in writing or printed, or in part both, to be signed by the clerk of said village, upon either owner or occupant of such land or lot, in case said owner or occupant resides in said village; and if neither said owner or occupant are residents of said village, then said order or notice shall be served by posting the same in three public places in said village, and placing the same in some conspicuous place on said lot, describing particularly the improvement to be made, manner in which the same is ordered to be done, and the materials which shall be used, and the quality thereof, if they deem proper, and setting forth the time in which the same shall be completed; and, in case the said improvement shall not be made and completed within the time and in the manner prescribed in such order or notice, the said trustees may cause such improvement to be made or completed in the manner specified in such order or notice, and the expenses thereof, with ten per cent. thereno, may be by them assessed on such lots, respectively,

Trustees have power to make or improve sidewalks and to compel owners of land to make or improve sidewalks.

Mode of carrying this section into effect.

Notice to be served.

Service upon non-residents.

Trustees to make improvements if owners refuse.

Expenses thereof to be a lien.

and shall be a lien thereon, and may be collected as is in this charter provided. It shall be the duty of the owner or occupant of any land or lots adjoining any street or highway in said village, at all times and without service on such owner or occupant of any notice or order to keep the sidewalks on the streets and highways within said village, in front of or adjoining said land or lots, at all times free and clear of snow, ice or other materials; and in case any owner or occupant shall neglect so to do, it shall be the duty of said trustees forthwith to cause the same to be done; the expenses whereof, with ten per cent. thereon, may be by them assessed on such lots, respectively, and shall be a lien thereon, and may be collected as in this charter provided.

Owners or occupants of land to keep their sidewalks clear of snow, ice, &c.

Trustees may enforce same.

Mode of Collecting Assessments.

Sale of lands for unpaid street, sewer, or sidewalk assessments.

§ 12. In the collection of all assessments made in opening streets, or in making other public improvements, or made for paving any street or portion thereof, or building a public sewer therein, or made for making, paving, grading, repairing or keeping clean any sidewalk as in this charter provided, the board of trustees may enforce the lien thereof on any premises, by sale, as provided for the collection of unpaid taxes, or may bring an action for the same, adding all percentage allowed by this act, in any court of this state having jurisdiction, or may prosecute for the same before the police justice of this corporation, and shall be entitled to all the remedies and process in said action, or before said police justice, as is provided in this act for the collection of unpaid taxes, or they may include the amount of such assessment in next tax list against the person so assessed, and such remedies may be resorted to in the same manner as is provided herein, in the collection or enforcement of unpaid taxes.

Assessments may be collected by suit or reassessment.

Streets and Public Squares to be Recorded.

Streets and squares to be recorded.

§ 13. The board of trustees shall cause such of the streets, public lanes, alleys, highways and public squares in said village, or any part thereof, as shall have been heretofore laid out, but not recorded or sufficiently described, and such as shall have been used for twenty years, but not recorded, to be ascertained, described and entered on record in a book to be kept by the clerk of the said village.

Street Commissioner shall Superintend Work.

§ 14. The working, paving, improving, cleaning and repairing the streets shall be performed under the superintendence of the street commissioner, who shall be always subject to the direction of the trustees in the discharge of his official duties, and no account for the expenditure on the streets shall be paid until the same shall be audited by the board of trustees, and a warrant or order drawn therefor on the treasury by the president, countersigned by the clerk; and all payments shall be made upon vouchers to be furnished and signed by the street commissioner, who shall himself pay out no moneys, which shall contain the name of the person, and the service or other thing for which the payment is made.

Duties of street commissioner.

Accounts how audited and paid.

Definition of Street.

§ 15. The word "street," as used in this act, shall be deemed to comprehend all parks, public squares, highways, streets, lanes and alleys within the corporation.

Definition of "street."

TITLE VIII.

AUDITING AND PAYMENT OF DEBTS.

Board of Trustees shall Audit.

SECTION 1. The board of trustees shall audit and pass upon all claims and demands against this corporation and, may allow the whole or part of any claim, or disallow it entirely, as herein provided. No claim or demand shall be allowed or audited unless the money to pay the same

Trustees to audit claims.

Payments how made.

shall have been voted by the village meeting, or unless the board of trustees shall have power under this charter to raise a tax for such purpose without such vote, and no claim or demand shall be paid unless audited and allowed as by this charter provided.

Manner of Presenting, Auditing and Proving Claims.

Warrants how drawn upon treasurer.

§ 2. Upon the auditing of claims against said village by the board of trustees, a warrant for the amount thereof shall be drawn upon the treasurer, to be signed by the acting president, which shall be paid by the treasurer, and filed in his office; but no account or claim against such village shall be paid until it shall have been presented to the trustees thereof, and audited and allowed by them; and when any such account or claim shall be so audited, the trustees auditing the same shall indorse thereon or annex thereto a certificate, subscribed by them, of such auditing, and of the allowing or disallowing the same, in which the sum allowed, if any, and the charges for which the same was allowed, shall be specified.

Accounts not to be paid unless audited.

Certificate to be annexed.

Claims—How Made Out.

Accounts to be made out in items and verified.

§ 3. No such account or claim shall be audited or allowed by the trustees unless it shall be made out in items, and shall be accompanied with an affidavit of the person claiming to have done the services or made the disbursements therein charged; that the several items of such account or claim are correct; that the services therein charged have been rendered; that the disbursements therein charged have been made, and that no part thereof has been paid. Such affidavit shall be endorsed on or annexed to such account or claim and presented and preserved therewith. The president or trustee presiding, when such account or claim shall be presented to the trustees, may administer the oath required by this section; and the trustees may examine the claimant on oath as to any items embraced in such account or claim.

Trustees may examine claimant under oath.

Disallowing Accounts.

§ 4. Nothing in the last preceding section shall be construted to prevent the trustees from disallowing any account or claim, in whole or in part, when so made out and verified, nor from requiring other or further evidence of the correctness and reasonableness thereof. Trustees may disallow or require further evidence.

Numbering Accounts.

§ 5. Every account or claim against said village, presented to the trustees in any year, shall be numbered from number one upwards in the order in which it shall be presented; and a memorandum of the time of presenting the same, the name of the person in whose favor it shall be made out, and of the person by whom it shall be presented, shall be entered in the records of the proceedings of the trustees. Accounts must be numbered and entered in records.

Form of Warrant.

§ 6. Every warrant drawn by the trustees, to pay any account or claim shall refer to such account by its number, the name of the person in whose favor it was made out, and the time when it was presented; and a memorandum of such reference, and of the amount of the warrant, shall be entered in such records before such warrant shall be delivered to the claimant. Warrant what to contain.

Requisites of Warrants.

§ 7. No payment shall be made by the treasurer from any money belonging to such village, except upon the warrant of the president of the board of trustees duly certified, indorsed on or annexed to the account or claim for which it shall be drawn, and specifying the fund from which it is payable, nor unless such account or claim shall appear by a certificate indorsed thereon or annexed thereto, and signed by the trustees, to have been audited and allowed by them; and when such warrant shall be paid, Treasurer to make payments on warrant. Warrant to designate fund from which payable.

Warrant to be filed.

the treasurer shall file and keep the same, together with the papers presented to him therewith, as required by this act.

Trustees or Officers personally liable.

Personal liability of trustees for creating debts, etc.

§ 8. If any member of the board of trustees, or other officer of this village, shall in any way assume to create a debt, or incur any liability on account of or against this village, or to appropriate or pay any money, or to use or apply any property or thing of value belonging to this village, for any purpose or in any manner whatsoever, contrary to the provisions of this charter, he shall be deemed guilty of a misdemeanor, and be proceeded against as provided by the revised statutes of this state, and he shall also be personally liable to any person injured for such debt or property or thing of value thus misapplied, or for any debt or liability thus attempted to be incurred, and he shall in like manner be personally liable to this village for any amount of such debt or liability that it shall for any reason pay or assume to pay, and for any property or thing of value thus misapplied, or for any damages that may accrue to said village. Any person thus injured, or this village, may prosecute for any violation of this section in any court of civil jurisdiction in this state.

Penalty for violations.

Who may prosecute.

TITLE IX.

MISCELLANEOUS.

Inhabitants not incompetent as Jurors.

Competency of inhabitants as jurors, witnesses, etc.

SECTION 1. No person shall be deemed incompetent as judge, juror, justice, witness, sheriff or constable, in any suit, cause or proceeding in which the corporation shall be a party, by reason of his being an inhabitant of the said village.

Voters not to be Arrested on Civil Process on Election Day.

§ 2. No person entitled to vote at any election held under this act shall be arrested on any civil process within the said village, on the day on which such election is held. Freedom from civil arrest on election day.

No Debt to be made.

§ 3. No debt shall be incurred or created by the said village, by the trustees, or by any other officer thereof, in their official capacity; nor shall the trustees, or any one or more of them, or any other officer of the corporation, be interested in any job or contract to which the said corporation shall be a party; nor shall any expenditure be made or incurred until the money or tax for that specific object shall have been voted as herein directed; nor shall the credit of the said corporation or its bonds or other obligations be loaned to any individual or to any other corporation; nor shall the corporation hereby created subscribe to or take stock as a corporate body in any work, project or enterprise or company whatever, except as herein provided, or as provided by the statutes or laws of this state. No officer shall create a debt or be interested in any contract. Expenditures shall not be incurred till tax is voted. Credit of the village shall not be loaned.

All Fines to belong to the Village.

§ 4. All moneys which shall be collected on account of taxes, or received for licenses, fines, penalties or forfeitures under this act, shall belong to said corporation, and shall be paid into the treasury thereof, excepting the fees of collection as hereinbefore provided. Taxes, licenses and fines to belong to the village.

Offices of Overseers of Highways Abolished.

§ 5. The offices of overseers of highways, and also all assessment of highway work to be paid in labor within the orporation, are abolished. Highway labor abolished.

* * * * * *

Cattle Running at Large Unlawful.

Allowing animals to run at large unlawful.

§ 7. It shall be unlawful for any cattle, horses, swine, geese or other animal to run at large upon any of the streets of this village, or to trespass or go upon any of the public parks, cemeteries, or other public grounds thereof. Any person may, and it shall be the duty of the pound keeper to, take up any cattle, horses, swine, geese or other animal which may be found thus doing damage or running at large, and put them immediately in the pound, without first confining them in any other place, and may then proceed to recover the damage which has been done by any such animals, or the penalties incurred by their running at large, as the case may be, in such manner as shall be provided by the by-laws of the corporation ; and it shall be the duty of the pound master to receive any such animal, and detain it in the pound until it shall be discharged from such impounding by due process of law

Such animals to be impounded.

Damages to be recovered.

Docks on Lake. *

Docks and other erections in Seneca Lake, in front of any street, prohibited.

Penalty.

§ 8. No person shall erect or put any building, wharf, dock or other fixture in the Seneca lake, in front of any street extending to the lake, except as hereinafter provided. Whoever shall offend against this provision, shall forfeit, for each offense, fifty dollars, and shall also forfeit ten dollars for each day such building, wharf, dock or fixture shall remain in said lake in front of each street, after receiving notice from the trustees to remove the same ; and, for the purpose of defining what part of the lake is in front of any such street, the line of such streets respectively, shall unless the same shall have been lawfully determined otherwise, be deemed to extend into the lake, without any alteration of their course , provided, however, that such extension, in the direction aforesaid, shall not conflict with private rights already lawfully acquired.

Proviso.

---

*Chap. 623 Laws of 1874.—§ 8, Section six of title nine of said act is hereby repealed.

§ 9. It shall be lawful for the trustees of said village to authorize and control the erection of wharves, docks and other fixtures in Seneca lake in front of streets running to said lake, as the interests and convenience of the people of said village may require, but in such manner as shall not obstruct the free navigation of said lake, provided that nothing herein contained shall interfere with any private right lawfully acquired.

Power of trustees as to erection of such docks.

Navigation not to be obstructed.

Officers not to be Interested in Contract.

§ 10. No member of the board of trustees shall in any way, either directly or indirectly, be interested in any contract with this corporation or in any work done or to be done for this corporation, by its officers, employees, or otherwise, except to see that such contract is faithfully carried out by all parties, and that such work is honestly done, and no other officer of this corporation (except members of the fire department, or extra police, or night watch who hold no other village office) shall, in any way, either directly or indirectly, be pecuniarily interested in any contract, or in any work done or to be done for this village, nor, beyond his fees, salary or pay allowed or authorized by this charter, shall he in any way receive any benefit or emolument therefrom, except as above stated. Any member of the board of trustees, or other officers, who shall violate the provisions of this section, or any of them, shall be guilty of a misdemeanor, triable by the police justice or any court of criminal jurisdiction in Ontario county, on the complaint of any inhabitant of this village, such crime to be punished as provided by the revised statutes of this state for misdemeanors.

No officer to be interested in any contract.

Penalty for violation thereof.

Officers to deliver Books to Successors.

§ 11. If any person having been an officer in said village shall not, within ten days after notification and request, deliver to his successor in office all the property, papers and effects, of every description, in his possession, or under his control, belonging to the said village, or ap-

Penalty for refusing to deliver records, papers, etc., to successor in office.

pertaining to his office, he shall forfeit and pay, for the use of the village, fifty dollars, besides all damage caused by his neglect or refusal to deliver.

Double Costs to Officers.

Officers when to recover double costs. § 12. Every person now or hereafter elected or appointed under this act to any office, who shall be sued for any act done, or omitted to be done, under such election or appointment, and any person who shall be sued for any act or thing done by the command of any officer, shall, if final judgment be rendered thereon, whereby any such defendant shall be entitled to costs, recover double costs, as defined by the revised statutes.

President and Clerk may Administer Oaths.

President and clerk may administer oaths. § 13. The president of the village and clerk shall have power to administer any oath authorized and required to be taken by this act, except where it is especially provided otherwise by this act.

President Must Execute Papers.

President to execute licenses, etc. § 14. All licenses, drafts, instruments or papers to be executed as the acts of the village, or in the transaction of its business affairs, except as otherwise provided in this act, may be executed by the president of said village, under the corporate seal.

How Suits to be Brought.

Suits, how brought by village. § 15. All suits brought for the recovery of any fine, penalty or forfeiture prescribed by the laws of this state by this act, or by any by-law made by virtue thereof, may be brought in the name of said corporation, and the pleadings and proceedings shall be the same as prescribed by the code of procedure of this state; either party may give this act, the said by-laws, and any special matter in evidence, and the party in whose favor judgment shall be rendered shall recover costs and have execution of such judgment in like manner as in other cases, unless otherwise in this act provided

Guardians for Infants to be Appointed in Suits.

§ 16. In all proceedings in any court, when there are infants or other incompetent persons, owners, whose property is affected by such proceedings, such court shall appoint guardians ad litem, to protect their interest, with the usual powers, and subject to all the duties of guardian ad litem in ordinary suits. Appointment of guardians ad litem.

Votes by Yeas and Nays.

§ 17. On demand of any member of the board of trustees the vote of such board on any matter shall be taken by yeas and nays, to be included in the minutes and entered upon the records Record of votes by yeas and nays.

Evidence of Records and Proceedings.

§ 18. All entries in the journal and in the clerk's minutes, or copies thereof, duly certified by the clerk, and the corporate seal thereto annexed, shall, for every purpose, be evidence in all courts of this state of the facts therein stated. Clerk's minutes and copies how used in evidence.

§ 19. The clerk of the village shall make and sign an entry or record, in a book to be provided for that purpose, of every ordinance and by-law enacted by the board of trustees, and of the time of publication thereof; and the said record, or a copy thereof, certified by the clerk of said village, shall be presumptive evidence in all courts and places of the due passage of such ordinances and by-laws, and of their having been duly published. Clerk to record ordinances and by-laws. To be presumptive evidence.

Exemptions of Firemen.

§ 20. Every member of the fire department shall, so long as he shall remain such member, be exempt from Exemption of firemen from jury and military duty and poll tax.

serving on juries in any court, and from paying any poll tax, and from serving in the militia, excepting in cases of invasion or insurrection, and every person who shall serve in such fire department five years successively, including the time he shall have served continually as a fireman in said village before the passing of this act, shall thereafter be entitled to the like exemption of military service, and a certificate of such service in the fire department, with a copy of this section, authenticated by the signature of the president and the seal of the corporation, shall be legal evidence before all courts and officers, civil or military of such exemption.

Persons must Aid at Fires.

Inhabitants disobeying orders, etc., at fires to forfeit penalty.

§ 21. Any inhabitant of this village who shall at the time of any fire refuse to obey the order of the president or chief engineer, or any person who shall at the time of any fire be guilty of any mutinous or disorderly conduct, or who shall attempt to excite mutiny, disorder or insubordination in others, or who shall obstruct or attempt to obstruct the operation of the fire department, or any member thereof, in the proper execution of his duties, or the orders of the proper officers, or who shall interfere with the engines, hose, or other property of this village, unless requested by some proper officer then having charge of the same, shall for each such offense forfeit such penalty as shall be prescribed by the by-laws, not exceeding fifty dollars.

Disorderly Persons.

Who to be deemed disorderly persons.

§ 22. All persons who shall be intoxicated in any street, park, alley, or public place in said village, and all persons who shall, by noisy, tumultuous, or riotous conduct, disturb the people; and all persons who shall have incited or induced dogs to fight, or be engaged in exciting and causing them to fight, in any street or public place in the village; and all persons who shall fight on any street or public square in the village; and all persons who shall, by blowing horns, hallooing, or otherwise make loud noises, tending to disturb the quiet of the people without just cause; and all persons who shall break or injure any awning or awning-post, or any public lamp or lamp-post, or shall wilfully and for the purpose of disturbance or mischief, give or create any false alarm of fire, or remove from or pile up before any door, boxes, casks, or other things, for the purpose of annoyance and mischief; and all persons who shall wilfully throw ink, or other liquid, or any missile or thing, upon or against any building of the village, or through any window thereof; and any person who shall wilfully break, injure, or deface any fence, trees, shrubbery, or ornamental thing in the village, are hereby declared disorderly persons, and may be proceeded against according to the provision of this act. Persons charged with any of the offenses specified in this section, which is by the existing law a crime or misdemeanor, may be proceeded against before the police justice according to the present provisions of law. **How proceeded against.**

How Tried and Punished.

§ 23. The police justice shall have power in cases of persons brought before him, within the meaning of this act, to proceed summarily and without a jury to try such persons, and hear and determine the charges alleged against them—and in case any person shall be found guilty of any such acts or offenses as constitute him a disorderly person within the meaning of this act, such police justice shall impose upon him a fine not exceeding fifty dollars, and sentence him to stand committed to the common jail of the county (or to such penitentiary as the said police justice may be authorized to commit persons to) until the same be paid not excceeding sixty-five days, or he may sentence him to be confined in the county jail, not to exceed three months. **Powers of police justice to proceed summarily.** **How published.** **Chap. 163, laws of 1862.** **Sentence.**

Terms of Officers in Office.

§ 24. The several persons elected at the last charter election in said village shall hold and discharge the duties **Present officers to continue in office.**

of the offices to which they were severally elected for and during the term for which they were so elected, the same as though this act had not been passed; and the several persons who have been appointed to any office in said village shall continue to hold and perform the duties of such offices, respectively, for and during the time for which they were so appointed, unless the person so elected or appointed shall be removed; and the provisions of this act shall be applicable to all the officers of said village so elected or appointed.

Repeal of Former Laws.

Repeal of former charter.

Proviso.

§ 25. From and after the passage of this act all former acts relating to said village of Geneva, as a corporation, and which are charters of the same, or amendments of such charters, are hereby repealed. But such appeal shall not affect any right vested or established, or any suit; proceeding or prosecution had or commenced, previous to the passage of this act, but every such right, suit or proceeding shall remain as valid and effectual as if such previous act had remained in force; and all estates, real and personal, vested in or belonging to the village of Geneva, when this act shall take effect, shall continue to be vested in and belong to said village.

This charter a public act.

§ 26. This act shall be deemed a public act, and the legislature may at any time repeal, modify or alter the same.

Publication.

§ 27. This act shall be published as the trustees shall direct within forty days after its passage.

§ 28. This act shall take effect immediately.

CHAPTER 265—Passed April 23, 1883.

TITLE X.

SECTION 1. The corporation known and created as "the trustees of the village of Geneva" is hereby authorized and empowered to create and issue its bonds to an amount not exceeding the sum of seventy-five thousand dollars, for the purpose and in the manner hereinafter provided. Such bonds shall all be dated at the same time, and be signed by the president of the village and countersigned by the clerk thereof. They shall be numbered consecutively, beginning from number one. They shall be under the corporate seal of said "the trustees of the village of Geneva." They may be payable at a particular place or generally to bearer, or to the same person or bearer or to same person or order; they shall bear interest at a rate not exceeding the lawful rate of interest at the date of their issue, payable once in each year, or in installments twice in each year, and may have coupons attached for interest to accrue thereon, or may be without coupons. If coupons are attached to such bonds they shall correspond in number and amounts with the several payments of interest to become due on their respective bonds, and shall be signed and countersigned in like manner as such bonds. The said bonds shall, as soon as they are signed, countersigned and sealed, and before they are issued, be registered by the clerk in a book to be provided and kept especially for that purpose, and as soon as any bond is issued there shall be entered on the said registry the name of the person to whom it is issued. The registry thereof shall show the numbers and amount of such bonds and the time when payable, and whether with coupons attached or not, and if payable to any person or bearer or to any person or order, the person to whom so payable and the time when interest is payable thereon and the rate per centum thereof. And when any of said bonds or coupons or the interest on any of said bonds, are or is paid or otherwise redeemed, an entry of that fact shall be made on said

Corporation may issue bonds.

How issued.

To be registered.

registry book opposite the registry of said bond or bonds. The said bonds may be for any sum of principal not less than fifty dollars each and not more than one thousand dollars each, and shall be made payable at different times and as follows: Three thousand seven hundred and fifty dollars thereof one year after the date thereof, four thousand dollars thereof two years after the date thereof, four thousand two hundred and fifty dollars thereof three years after the date thereof, four thousand six hundred dollars thereof four years after the date thereof, four thousand nine hundred and fifty dollars thereof five years after the date thereof, five thousand two hundred and fifty dollars thereof six years after the date thereof, five thousand six hundred dollars thereof seven years after the date thereof, six thousand and fifty dollars thereof eight years after the date thereof, six thousand four hundred and fifty dollars nine years after the date thereof, six thousand eight hundred and fifty dollars ten years after the date thereof, seven thousand four hundred dollars thereof eleven years after the date thereof, seven thousand nine hundred dollars thereof in twelve years from the date thereof, and seven thousand nine hundred and fifty dollars thereof in thirteen years from the date thereof. Such bonds shall not be sold or in any manner disposed of except as hereinafter provided.

Denomination.

When payable.

§ 2. The corporation known and created as "the trustees of the village of Geneva," is hereby authorized to subscribe in and by its corporate name for and take shares in the capital stock of the Geneva and Southwestern Railway Company, a railroad corporation chartered under the general laws of this State, to the number of not more than seven hundred and fifty of the par value of one hundred dollars each, in the aggregate to the amount of not more than seventy-five thousand dollars, and it may at any time sell and dispost of said stock or any part thereof, not however for less than its par value, and the proceeds of such sales and any dividends or the proceeds thereof received on said stock, shall be paid to the treasurer of said "the

Trustees may subscribe for and take stock in G. & S. W. Railway Co.

trustees of the village of Geneva," to be by him held and applied to the payment of the principal and interest of the bonds provided for in section one of this title as hereinafter directed.

§ 3. The said corporation, "the trustees of the village of Geneva," is hereby authorized and empowered to pay for said stock by exchanging the bonds provided for in section one of this title therefor, dollar for dollar of the par value of said bonds and stock respectively, or by and with the proceeds of the sale of such bonds as provided for in the next section of this title and in no other manner. To pay for stock by exchange of bonds.

§ 4. The said corporation, "the trustees of the village of Geneva," is hereby authorized and empowered to sell and dispose of the bonds provided for in section one of this title, not, however, for a less rate than the par value thereof and the accrued interest thereon, and the par value thereof at the date of such sale, and to invest the proceeds of such sales in the stock of said, "the Geneva and South-western Railway Company," to an amount and at the rate provided for in section two of this title, but neither said bonds nor any of them, or the proceeds thereof or the interest thereon or the proceeds thereof shall be applied for or to any other purpose or purposes whatever. Bonds not to be sold below par

§ 5. The board of trustees of said "the trustees of the village of Geneva," shall, every year, and until the bonds provided for in section one of this title, and all interest thereon are fully paid and redeemed, and at the usual time of the levy and assessment of taxes for the other purposes of said corporation; and in addition to such levy and assessment, and in connection therewith, levy, impose and assess a tax upon the taxable property within said corporation in addition to the amount voted at the annual tax meeting of the tax payers of the village of Geneva, a tax in an amount over and above all the expenses of the collection thereof, which, when added to that amount so voted at such tax meeting, will produce a sum no greater Tax to pay bonds. Total annual village tax not

To exceed one per cent. on assessed valuation of 1872.

than one per cent. of the assessed value of the taxable property within such corporation according to the assessment roll of eighteen hundred and seventy-two, so that the whole amount of tax levied and assessed in any one year on the property within such corporation shall be one per cent. of the assessed value of the taxable property within such corporation in the year eighteen hundred and seventy-two, exclusive of an amount over and above all the expenses of the collection thereof; and also exclusive of an amount sufficient to pay all salaries fixed by the charter and by-laws of said corporation ; and also exclusive of any amount heretofore or hereafter raised or voted, or to be raised or voted or to pay any debt or the interest thereon, heretofore created or hereafter to be created under and by virtue of section twelve of title six of an act to revise and consolidate the laws in relation to the village of Geneva, in the county of Ontario, passed March third, eighteen hundred and seventy-one, and no more. The said tax shall be levied, assessed and collected and paid into the treasury of said corporation, "the trustees of the village of Geneva," in the same manner as is provided by law for the levy, assessment and collection of other taxes authorized to be levied, assessed and collected by said corporation.

Exceptions.

Proceeds of Railway stock to be applied in payment of village bonds.

§ 6. It shall be the duty of the treasurer of said "the trustees of the village of Geneva," to set apart and place to a separate account all moneys which may arise from a sale of any of the stock of said "the Geneva and Southwestern Railway Company," or for interest or dividend thereon, or the proceeds thereof and apply the same, from time to time, to the payment of said bonds and the interest thereon, as the same shall become due, and it shall also be his duty to set apart out of the first moneys paid into the treasury of said corporation, "the trustees of the village of Geneva," in each year by the collector of said corporation, and place to the same account, and apply in the same manner the sum of nine thousand dollars.

Trustees to report at annual tax meeting.

§ 7. At every annual tax meeting of the tax payers of the village of Geneva, held in pursuance of the charter thereof, the board of trustees of said. "the trustees of the village of Geneva." shall report to such meeting, in writing, how much stock has been subscribed for by virtue of this title. how much is then held and owned by said corporation, how much has been paid for assessment thereon and received in dividends therefrom, how much has, up to that time, been sold, and for what price, and how the moneys received therefor have been disposed of, how much in amount of said bonds have been issued, and to whom and when, and how much money has been received therefor and how disposed of. how many in amount have been paid, with the numbers thereof, how much interest has been paid on said bonds and how many in amount still remain unpaid.

§ 8. It shall be competent for the trustees of the village of Geneva to enter into any agreement. in writing, with "the Geneva and Southwestern Railway Company," limiting and defining the time when and the proportions in which the bonds provided for in section one of this title shall be delivered or the proceeds thereof paid to the said "the Geneva and Southwestern Railway Company," and the place or places where, and the purposes for which said bonds or their proceeds shall be applied or used ; and any such agreement in writing, duly executed by such railway company and said "the trustees of the village of Geneva." shall, in all courts and places, be valid and effectual, and said "the trustees of the village of Geneva" shall not be compelled by any court or required by law to deliver said bonds or pay over the proceeds thereof to said railway company, or make any payment on account of its subscription to the stock of said railway company until such agreement shall have been executed, if required, by said "the trustees of the village of Geneva." Agreement as to time of delivery of bonds.

§ 9. Nothing contained in section one of title six, or in section three of title nine of "An act to revise and consolidate the laws in relation to the village of Geneva, in the county of Ontario," passed March third, eighteen hundred and seventy-one, shall be construed to require the Tax authorized by this act not to be voted at tax meeting.

tax directed to be levied, assessed and collected by this act, or the expenditure thereof as directed by this act, to be authorized by a vote of the taxable inhabitants of this village.

Provisions of this act mandatory.

§ 10. All the provisions in this act contained, shall be construed as mandatory and not as directory, so far as to make the sevaral officers of said corporation, said "the trustees of the village of Geneva," who may have any duties to perform under this act, liable for all neglect or misfeasance or malfeasance.

§ 2. This act shall take effect immediately.

TITLE XI.

Chap. 163, laws of 1882.

Police commissioners to serve without pay; term of office.

SECTION 1. Samuel H. Ver Planck, Francis O. Mason aud Philip N. Nicholas, resident taxpayers of the village of Geneva, upon taking the constitutional oath of office, shall be and hereby are constituted a board of police commissioners of the village of Geneva, who shall serve, without pay, for two, four and six years, respectively, said terms of office to be determined by said commissioners by lot within thirty days after the passage of this act, and each two years thereafter the board of trustees of the village of Geneva, shall appoint one commissioner, who shall be a resident tax payer of the village of Geneva, to serve for a full term of six years, and until his successor is appointed; and the said village board may at any time appoint to fill a vacancy occurring in said board of commissioners for the unexpired term. Said commissioners or any of them, or their successors, may be removed for neglect to perform their prescribed duties, or for official malfeasance of any kind by a two-thirds vote of said village board; but prior to such removal, written charges shall be preferred by at least a majority of said village board, and an opportunity to answer in person shall be given. Said charges must be preferred against individual members of the board of police commissioners, and not against the board as a whole.

Power of removal upon written charges

§ 2. The said police commissioners shall take the constitutional oath of office, and shall elect their own presiding officer. They shall appoint from their own number a clerk, whose duty it shall be to keep a record of all appointments and removals made by them under this act, as hereinafter contained, and also of the acts and regulations done or enacted by them as said board of police commissioners, which said record shall at all times be open to the inspection of the board of trustees and of the town board.

To take oath; to appoint a clerk who is to keep the records.

§ 3. The board of police commissioners shall appoint such number of policemen as shall be fixed by the board of trustees of the village of Geneva, not to exceed six who shall constitute the police force of said village, who shall hold office during good behavior, except as hereinafter provided, and who shall take and file with the clerk of the village of Geneva the constitutional oath of office before entering upon the duties of his office. A certificate of the appointment of such policemen shall be duly filed with the clerk of the village of Geneva, and a copy thereof, duly certified by said clerk, shall be filed in the office of the clerk of Ontario county.

Chap. 294, laws of 1886.

To appoint police, who shall hold office during good behavior.

§ 4. One of such policemen shall be designated by the board of police commissioners as "chief of police," who shall perform such duties as shall be prescribed by law, or by the lawful rules and regulations of the board of police commissioners.

Chief of police.

§ 5. In case of a vacancy in said police force for any cause, the said board of police commissioners shall appoint to fill the vacancy; and they may remove any of said policemen upon being convinced of their incompetency, or of their being guilty of illegal, corrupt or other improper conduct.

Commissioners to fill vacancies in police force.

§ 6. The said policemen shall have the full power and duties of constables of towns in regard to criminal process and proceedings, and in addition thereto all the powers and duties conferred by the charter of the village of

Chap. 294, laws of 1886.

Powers and duties of the police.

Geneva upon police constables, except in respect to civil process issued by any officer other than the police justice, and they shall perform such other duties as shall be lawfully prescribed by the rules and regulations of the board of police commissioners, and it shall be the duty of said policemen to serve any and all process and papers issued by the police justice of the village of Geneva, and no other officer or person shall have the authority to serve such process and papers, except where, in the opinion of the police justice, the service can be more efficiently performed by a town constable; and this discretion shall apply only to those cases arising without the corporate limits of the village, and it shall not be competent for any constable or deputy sheriff to make arrests within the village without warrants, except in cases of breach of the peace or other crimes, while actually occurring. But no limitations of the powers of constables or deputy sheriffs shall apply to any special police, or to those special deputy sheriffs appointed under an act passed April twelve, eighteen hundred and sixty seven (being chapter three hundred and seventy-five of the laws of eighteen hundred and sixty-seven.

Chap. 411, laws of 1889.

§ 7. The pay of said policemen shall from time to time be fixed by the police commissioners, but shall not exceed the rate of sixty dollars per month for the time actually served, except that the pay of the policeman designated as "chief of police" may in the discretion of the commisioners be increased to seventy-five dollars per month. Such salaries shall be paid monthly from any unappropriated money in the treasury of the village of Geneva. Such policemen shall not receive any other compensation, except when traveling in discharge of their duty in conveying persons to prison, or by direction of the police commissioners, in the discharge of their duty, or when attending on behalf of the people as witnesses before the grand jury or before any court within the county upon investigations or prosecutions for crime, charged to have been committed within the village of Geneva, when their actual expenses

Pay of Policemen.

shall be paid, upon a verified account of the items of such expense in detail, to be certified by the board of police commissioners, and audited and paid by the board of trustees out of unappropriated moneys aforesaid.

§ 8. Each of the said policemen shall keep a correct account of such services rendered by him as have heretofore been a town or county charge, and such accounts duly verified and sworn to by such policemen, shall be presented by the police commissioners at least once a year to the proper town or county auditing boards; which accounts shall be a charge against the town or county, as if made by a town constable as heretofore, and when audited by said town or county boards, shall be paid to the treasurer of the village of Geneva, for the use of said village. Except that no extra compensation shall be charged against the town for "care of prisoners," which said care shall be a part of the duty of said police and only such drawback for meals for prisoners shall be allowed against the town as shall have been actually expended in furnishing such meals at the lowest attainable rate.

Police to render bills against town and county.

To make no charge for care of prisoners; to be paid the actual cost of meals.

APPENDIX;

CONTAINING ACTS OF THE LEGISLATURE APPLICABLE TO THE VILLAGE OF GENEVA.

WATER WORKS.

CHAPTER 63—passed March 31, 1803.

AN ACT to incorporate the proprietors of the Geneva Water Works.

The incorporators named in the act are Jacob Hallett, Herman H. Bogert, Jacob W. Hallett, Samuel Colt, Nathaniel Merrill, David Cook, David Naglee, Ezra Patterson, Charles Williamson, Thomas Powell, John Johnston, Polydore B. Wisner and Joseph Annin.

CEMETERIES.

CHAPTER 727.

AN ACT authorizing cities and villages to acquire title to property for burial purposes, and to levy taxes for the payment of the same. Passed May 8, 1869.

CHAPTER 760.

AN ACT to amend chapter 727 of the laws of 1869, entitled "An act authorizing cities and villages to acquire title to property for burial purposes, etc." Passed May 9, 1870.

CHAPTER 696, LAWS OF 1871.

(Amending the foregoing acts.) Passed April 25, 1871.

SECTION 1. The trustees of any village are hereby authorized to appoint a cemetery commission of not less than five, nor more than nine resident freeholders of said village, who shall, during their term of office, have exclusive control and management of the laying out, beautifying and improving of any lands which may be purchased by said trustees as provided by section one of the act hereby amended. The members of such commission shall hold their office for five years from and after their appointment, and when vacancies occur in such commission the same shall be filled by said trustees from the resident freeholders of said villages. All moneys appropriated by said trustees for the improvement of such lands, shall be placed in the hands of said commission to be expended by them in such laying out, beautifying and improving; and said commission shall, on the *first day of March in each year* during their term of office, make a report by items of their expenditures, and stating the objects thereof, to said trustees, which report shall be in writing, signed by a majority of the members of such commission and verified by their oaths.

CHAPTER 629.

AN ACT for the protection of birds in public cemeteries. Passed July 21, 1853.

CHAPTER 180.

AN ACT for the protection of graves in cemeteries. Passed April 27, 1878; three-fifths being present.

SECTION 1. Hereafter it shall be a misdemeanor and be punishable as such, for any person other than the owner to remove from any grave in any cemetery in the State, any flowers or other memorial, or any token of affection placed on or near any such grave or any wire frame work or other thing in any way connected with such flowers, memorial or token.

§ 2. The provisions of this act shall not apply to the officers or employees of any of the cemetery associations of this state in the enforcement of the rules and regulations under which such associations may be governed, provided that all articles removed by them from graves shall be destroyed so that they cannot be again used.

CHAPTER 177.

AN ACT in relation to the establishment and care of a cemetery by the village of Geneva, Ontario county, and to provide means for the same. Passed April 6, 1872: three-fifths being present.

SECTION 1. The appointment heretofore made by the trustees of the village of Geneva, Ontario county, of Phineas Prouty, William E. Sill, Corydon Wheat, George W. Nicholas, Samuel S. Graves, George

B. Dusinberre, Thompson C. Maxwell, Stephen H. Parker and Angus Mc Donald, as cemetery commissioners, is hereby confirmed, notwithstanding that one of said commissioners, although a freeholder of said village, is not an actual resident therein.

§ 2. The said commissioners shall by lot divide themselves into three classes of three each. The term of office of one of said classes shall expire in five years, of another in six years, and of the third in seven years from the date of their appointment. Their successors shall be appointed by the trustees of the said village of Geneva, and shall each hold office for five years. Each commissioner shall hold office until his successor is appointed and has qualified. All vacancies shall be filled by like appointment for the unexpired term.

§ 3. In addition to the powers already conferred by law upon said commission, it shall have the exclusive power of conveying, by its chairman, to any person or persons, their heirs and assigns, for such consideration and upon such terms, conditions and under such restrictions as it may prescribe, the exclusive right to bury the dead and erect monuments in and upon any lands purchased or obtained by law by the trustees of the village of Geneva, for cemetery purposes, and shall have power to make contracts relating to such cemetery, and to enforce the same by suit brought in the name of "THE GENEVA CEMETERY COMMISSIONERS." [Chap. 450, laws of 1877.]

§ 4. The said commission shall also have the exclusive control and custody of all moneys which may be received from such sale of burial rights or otherwise from said lands under their control, and shall apply such portion of the same as it may think proper to the laying out, improving, beautifying and taking care of such lands, and the actual and necessary expenses of said commission, and the balance shall be applied in payment of any bonds which may be lawfully issued or liability which may be lawfully incurred by said trustees for the purchase, laying out, improving, beautifying and taking care of any lands for cemetery purposes.

§ 5. In case said balance of money is not sufficient to pay the bonds of said village issued to purchase, lay out, improve, beautify and take care of such lands for cemetery purposes, as they mature, the trustees of said village, may, on the written request of said commission, re-issue bonds of said village for an amount, and payable as stated in such request; but such re-issued bonds shall not exceed in amount the balance of such original bonds due and unpaid, and shall not be sold for less than par; and the avails shall be applied only in payment of said original bonds due and unpaid. Provided, however, that any portion of them may be exchanged for not less than an equal amount of said original bonds, and, provided further that no bonds re-issued under the provisions of this act shall be made payable more than ten years from the re-issue thereof.

CATTLE RUNNING AT LARGE.

CHAPTER 459, LAWS OF 1862.

AN ACT to prevent animals from running at large in the public highways. Passed April 23, 1862.

Amended by Chap. 814, passed May 9, 1867.
" Chap. 424, passed April 29, 1869.

The foregoing are further amended by Chap. 776, passed May 20, 1872, which act amends section one as follows:

SECTION 1. It shall not be lawful for any cattle, horses, sheep, swine or goats to run at large, or to be herded or pastured in any public street, park, place or highway in this State; and it shall be the duty of every overseer of highways within his road district, and of every street commissioner in any incorporated village, who shall have personal knowledge, or who shall be notified of any violation of this act, to sieze and to take into his possession, and to keep until disposed of according to law, any animal so found running at large or being herded or pastured, and any person suffering or permitting any animal to so run at large, or be herded or pastured in violation of this section, shall forfeit a penalty of five dollars for every horse, swine or cattle, and one dollar for every sheep or goat so found, to be recovered by civil action, by any inhabitant of the town in his own name, or in the name of the overseer of the poor of the town, or the proceedings hereinafter provided.

CHAPTER 345.

AN ACT in regard to publishing the accounts of incorporated villages in this State. Passed May 6, 1874.

As amended by Chap. 197. Passed April 29, 1875.

SECTION 1. It shall be the duty of the board of trustees, of each of the incorporated villages of this State, to cause to be published, once in each year and twenty days next before the annual meeting, in at least one public newspaper printed in such village or in a public newspaper that is, to all intents and purposes, a village newspaper of more than one village, and that has more than one publication office, one of which is in such incorporated village, a full and detailed account of all money received by them or the treasurer of said village for the account and use thereof, and of all money expended therefor, giving the items of expenditures in full. Should there be no paper published in said village, they shall be required to publish the same, by notice to the tax payers, by posting in five public places in said incorporated limits.

§ 2. Said annual report shall also state the funded and floating or temporary debt of said village.

CHAPTER 261.

AN ACT to prevent accident on railroads operated by steam power in the State of New York. Passed May 15, 1878; three-fifths being present.

SECTION 1. Any person or persons who shall get on or off a freight car or engine while in motion, or who shall ride on any wood or freight car, unless employed by or with permission from the proper officers of such railroad, or the person in charge of such car or engine, shall be deemed guilty of a misdemeanor, and shall be liable to a fine of twenty-five dollars or three months' imprisonment, or both fine and imprisonment.

CHAPTER 451.

AN ACT for the more effectual prevention of wanton and malicious mischief, and to prevent the defacement of natural scenery. Passed June 15, 1877.

SECTION 1. Any person who shall maliciously or wantonly injure or deface any monument or work of art, building, fence or other structure, or destroy or injure any ornamental tree, or shrub or plant, whether situated on any private ground or on any street, public or private way, or cemetery, or who shall paint or print upon, or in any other manner place upon or affix to any stone or rock, not a part of a building, or upon or to any bridge or tree, any word, letter, character or device, stating, referring to, or advertising, or intended to state, refer to or advertise the sale or manufacture of any property or article, profession, business, exhibition, amusement or place of amusement, or other thing, and any person who shall, directly or indirectly, cause any such act to be done, or shall aid therein, shall be deemed guilty of a misdemeanor, and upon conviction, shall, for each and every such offense, be punished by a fine not exceeding two hundred and fifty dollars, or by imprisonment not exceeding six months, or by both such fine and imprisonment.

§ 2. Provides in addition, for liability to owner of premises for damages.

§ 3. Provides that if actions under section one are not brought within six months, actions may be brought by overseer of the poor.

§ 4. The fact that such act has been aided or caused to be done by any person charged therewith, shall, in any such action, as a legal presumption, be deemed to be proved against any of the owners or proprietors or managers of the property, articles, profession, business, exhibition, amusement or other thing relative to which such words, letters, characters or devices may have been painted, printed, placed or affixed, as aforesaid, until the contrary is shown by competent evidence.

§ 5. Provides that action may be brought in justices' courts, etc.

CHAPTER 150.

AN ACT to enable the owners of lands on the shores of Seneca, Cayuga and Chatauque Lakes to erect wharves and storehouses on the lands covered with the waters of those lakes, adjacent to the lands owned by them. Passed April 2, 1827.

Be it enacted by the people of the State of New York, represented in Senate and Assembly, That it shall and may be lawful for David Brooks, his heirs and assigns, to build and erect a dock and storehouse in the Seneca Lake adjoining the lands now owned by said Brooks, known by the name of McKnight's Point, in the town of Romulus, in the county of Seneca.

And be it further enacted, That it shall and may be lawful for any person owning lands adjoining the Cayuga, Seneca or Chatauque lakes to erect any wharf or wharves, storehouse or storehouses, upon any land covered by the water of such lakes, adjacent to, and bounding upon the land of such owners; and to use, occupy and enjoy the same, as if conveyed by the commissioners of the land office, pursuant to an act passed February 6th, 1824.

Provided, That nothing in this act shall be so construed as to authorize any person to erect a wharf at the termination of any highway so as to obstruct the passage of ferry boats or any other water craft.

And provided further, That before any person or persons shall be authorized to erect any wharf or storehouse in Chatauque lake, such person or persons shall first apply to, and obtain the consent and order of the Court of Common Pleas of said county, which consent and order shall not be granted until the applicant or applicants shall first give at least three weeks notice of such intended application, by publishing a notice in one of the newspapers printed in said county; and when such order and consent shall be obtained, it shall forthwith be filed in the clerk's office of the county of Chatauque.

CHAPTER 219.

AN ACT *in relation to evidence in civil and criminal cases.* Passed May 7, 1878, as amended by chapter 211, passed April 25, 1879.

SECTION 1. Any act, ordinance, resolution, by-law, rule or proceeding of the common council of a city, or of the board of trustees of an incorporated village, or of a board of supervisors of any county within this state, and any recital of occurrences taking place at the sessions of any thereof, may be read in evidence on any trial, examination or proceeding, whether civil or criminal, either from a copy thereof certified by the clerk of the city, village, common council or board of supervisors or from a volume printed by authority of the common council of the city, or board of supervisors of the county, or of the board of trustees of any incorporated village.

CHAPTER 212.

AN ACT to establish the right of citizens of this state to carry on their business in all parts thereof. Passed May 3, 1878;
As amended by chapter 417, passed May 20, 1879.

SECTION 1. It shall not be lawful for the authorities of any county, city or village to impose upon the inhabitants of any other county, city or village within this State, carrying on or desiring to carry on any lawful trade, business or calling within the limits thereof, any restriction or condition whatever except such as may be necessary for the proper regulation of such trade, business or calling, and such as apply equally and impartially to the citizens of all parts of the State alike, and all ordinances in violation of the provisions of this act are hereby declared to be null and void. But the provisions of this act shall not apply to the ordinances or regulations of any county, city or village in this State in reference to traveling circuses, shows and exhibitions,

---

CHAPTER 353.

AN ACT in relation to taxation and incurring debt in incorporated villages. Passed May 25, 1881

This act provides that if a proposition to raise money or incur a debt for any purpose has been voted down by the tax payers. it shall not again be submitted to a vote until after the next annual election, "except when the necessity of the occasion for the same shall have arisen after the rejection of such resolution or proposition."

CHAPTER 226—MAY 9, 1881.

"AN ACT authorizing the board of trustees of any incorporated village, the trustees of any monument association or the town board of any town to acquire lands for monument purposes."

CHAPTER 226.

AN ACT to extend the time for the collection of taxes in the incorporated villages of this state. Passed May 27, 1882.

The People of the State of New York, represented in Senate and Assembly do enact as follows :

SECTION 1. It shall be lawful for any incorporated village in this state by its trustees to issue new warrants, or renew those which may be issued by them or their predecessors for the collection of any village tax, from time to time, as often as such warrants shall be returned uncollected, in whole or in part, during the term prescribed by its charter ; but the renewing of any such warrant shall in no way affect the liability of the collector or the sureties upon the bond of such collector.

§ 2. This act shall take effect immediately.

CHAPTER 113.

AN ACT in relation to alterations of highways, streets or bridges in incorporated villages. Passed March 16, 1883 : three-fifths being present.

The People of the State of New York, represented in Senate and Assembly, do enact as follows:

Section 1. Whenever the grade of any street, highway or bridge in any incorporated village in this state shall be changed or altered so as to interfere in any manner with any building or buildings situate thereon, or adjacent thereto, or the use thereof, or shall injure or damage the real property adjoining such highway so changed or altered, the owner or owners of such building or real estate may apply to the supreme court in the judicial district in which such property is situated for the appointment of three commissioners to ascertain and determine the amount of damage sustained thereby ; due notice of such application shall be given to the person or persons having competent authority to make such change or alteration.

§ 2. All the provisions of the general railroad act relative to the appointment of commissioners, their powers and duties, shall be applicable to the appointment of, and the powers and duties of commissioners appointed in pursuance of the provisions hereof.

§ 3. All damages ascertained and determined under the provisions of this act, together with the costs of such proceedings, shall be a charge upon the village, town or other municipality chargeable with the maintenance of the street, highway or bridge so altered or changed.

§ 4. This act shall take effect immediately.

CHAPTER 465.

AN ACT to authorize trustees of villages to regulate hawking, peddling and auctions. Passed May 25, 1883 ; three-fifths being present.

The People of the State of New York, represented in Senate and Assembly, do enact as follows:

Section 1. The trustees of any village in this state incorporated under special act of the legislature, and who have not the powers hereinafter conferred, shall, from and after the passage of this act, have power and authority to restrain, regulate or prevent hawking and peddling in the streets ; except the peddling and sale of meats, fish, fruits and farm produce, to regulate, restrain or prohibit sales by auction, and grant licenses to peddlers and auctioneers, and fix the amount to be paid therefor.

§ 2. This act shall take effect immediately.

CHAPTER 308.

AN ACT to confer additional powers upon the trustees and officers of incorporated villages in the state of New York. Passed May 19, 1884 ; three-fifths being present.

The People of the State of New York, represented in Senate and Assembly, do enact as follows:

SECTION 1. The trustees and officers of any village of this state created by special charter shall have and possess the same powers as are prescribed in any general act for the incorporation of villages within this state, except as such special charter may be in conflict with any provision or provisions of said general acts.

§ 2. This act shall take effect immediately.

CHAPTER 270.

AN ACT for the preservation of the public health, and the registration of vital statistics. Passed May 12, 1885; three-fifths being present.

The People of the State of New York, represented in Senate and Assembly, do enact as follows:

SECTION 1. * * * And it shall be the duty of the trustees of every incorporated village in this state to appoint once, in each year, a board of health of such village, to consist of not less than three nor more than seven persons (who are not village trustees), who shall hold office for one year, or until their successors shall have been appointed. The said board of health thus constituted shall elect a president, and appoint a competent physician (not a member of such board) to be the health officer of such village. * * *

CHAPTER 504—JUNE 2, 1887.

AN ACT conferring additional powers upon villages.

CHAPTER 371—MAY 20, 1890.

These acts provide for raising and expending, with the approval and consent of a majority vote of tax payers, an amount "additional to the amount permitted to be raised by its charter or by the general law aforesaid, for the purpose of building a bridge, constructing a sewer, or carrying out some other village object."

By a unanimous vote of the Board of Trustees they can raise and expend $500 without submitting the matter to the tax payers.

CHAPTER 244.

AN ACT to authorize the boards of trustees of villages incorporated under special charters to organize fire hook and ladder and hose companies, and fire departments therein, and to define the powers and duties thereof. Passed April 30, 1887.

SECTION 1. Provides that trustees of villages incorporated under special charters may organize fire companies, etc.

§ 2. "All persons who now are or hereafter shall become members of hose, hook and ladder or engine companies, not exceeding twenty-five members to each hose company and forty members to each hook and ladder or engine company of any such village incorporated as aforesaid, who after being duly elected by their respective companies and confirmed by the board of trustees of such village, shall be and hereby are ordained, constituted and declared to be a body corporate and politic in fact and in name by the name and style of the Fire Department of" * * *

§ 3. Annual meeting to recommend chief and assistant engineers.

§ 4 "The board of trustees of such village upon such recommendation shall appoint a chief engineer and two assistant engineers, who shall be electors of said village and who shall hold their offices during the pleasure of said board."

§ 5. Prescribes the duties of the chief engineer.

§ 6. Two fire wardens to be elected by each company, who with the chief and assistants shall constitute a council.

§ 7. Council to choose certain officers.

§ 8. Quorum of council—power of—public reviews.

§ 9. Failure to hold elections not to work dissolution.

§ 10. Annual meeting, time of.

§ 11. Time of service, how allowed.

§ 12. Certificate of full service, how signed.

SEWERAGE.

CHAPTER 375—JUNE 6, 1889.

AN ACT to provide for the construction of sewers in any incorporated village of this state.

CHAPTER 306—MAY 4, 1891.

CHAPTER 316—MAY 5, 1891.

Amends the preceding law.

These acts are quite lengthy but are of importance, and for full knowledge of them, reference must be made to the published session laws.

Their provisions are additional and supplementary to all other powers possessed by any incorporated village. Provision is made for a board of seven commissioners to be appointed by the village board of trustees. The commissioners are empowered to appoint one of their number president to serve without compensation; to appoint a clerk at a salary of $200; to make by-law; to employ an engineer and such other assistance as may be necessary, and procure a map and plan for a general or special system of sewerage which must be approved by the State Board of Health, the expense limited to $2,000, to be included in next annual tax levy.

Any portion of the plan adopted may be constructed and the whole or a portion of the expense may be apportioned upon the village at large, but subject to the approval of the taxpapers at a special election to be held after due notice is published. Assessments made upon lands benefitted to be a lien upon such property.

The commissioners may acquire necessary lands, may contract for the construction, and may issue bonds at five per cent interest, in such amount and upon such time as may be determined upon. The bonds to be delivered to, and sold by the village treasurer, who shall credit the receipts to a separate fund, called the sewer fund and who shall make payments upon orders signed by the president and countersigned by the clerk of the board of sewer commissioners. They shall have full charge of construction, maintenance and repairs.

CHAPTER 27—MARCH 11, 1890.

AN ACT to amend chapter 397 of the laws of 1873, entitled "An act for the incorporation of fire, hose, and hook and ladder companies."

Provides that any ten or more persons may be incorporated as a fire company, for a term not exceeding fifty years, with the consent of the board of trustees.

CHAPTER 525.

AN ACT to authorize incorporated villages to acquire lands for use as a public park.

Approved by the Governor June 8, 1888. Passed, three-fifths being present.

The People of the State of New York, represented in Senate and Assembly, do enact as follows:

SECTION 1. It shall be lawful for any incorporated village within the State to acquire by purchase, lease or gift, any lands within its corporate boundaries or adjacent thereto, or within one mile thereof to be used as a public park under control of the trustees of the village, and subject to such regulations as they may prescribe; but the total value of lands so acquired by any village shall not exceed three per cent of the assessed value of its taxable property; and whenever the board of trustees of any village shall have been previously authorized so to do, by a vote of the majority of the electors of the village voting thereon at any annual or special meeting duly called of such electors, they may acquire any lands for such purpose, and contract therefor, and caused to be raised by taxation upon the taxable property of the village, and by installments, if they shall see fit, such sum or sums as may be necessary to procure the title thereto, and annually thereafter such sums as may be necessary to meet the expense of the care, preservation and proper improvement of the lands acquired for the use aforesaid.

§ 2. This act shall take effect immediately.

CHATTER 812.

AN ACT to amend chapter four hundred and fifty-two of the laws of eighteen hundred and eighty-eight, entitled "An act to authorize and empower the board of trustees of incorporated villages in this state to contract with electric light companies, organized under the laws of this state for lighting the streets and public grounds of said villages."

Approved by the Governor, May 4, 1891. Passed, three-fifths being present.

The People of the State of New York, represented in Senate and Assembly, do enact as follows:

Section 1. Section one of chapter four hundred and fifty-two of the laws of eighteen hundred and eighty-eight, entitled "An act to authorize and empower the board of trustees of incorporated villages in this state to contract with electric light companies, organized under the laws of this state for lighting the streets and public grounds of said villages," is hereby amended so as to read as follows:

§ 1. The board of trustees of any incorporated village of this state, whether incorporated under the act entitled "An act for the incorporation of villages," passed April twentieth, eighteen hundred and seventy, and acts amendatory thereof and supplemental thereto, or by special charter or act, shall have the power and they are hereby authorized and empowered to contract for a term of one year or more with any electric light company, organized under the laws of this state, or with any person or persons, for lighting the streets and public grounds of such village; and the amount of such contract agreed to be paid shall be annually raised as a part of the expenses of such village, and shall be levied, assessed and collected in the manner that other expenses of said village are raised, and when collected shall be kept separate from other funds of said village, and shall be paid over to such electric light company, person or persons, by such trustees, according to the terms of any such contract ; and any such contract entered into by the board of trustees of any village shall be valid and binding upon such village, providing, however, that no such contract shall be made for a longer period than five years nor for a greater sum in the aggregate than one and one-half mills for every dollar of the taxable property of said village per annum, unless the proposition for the same be submitted to a vote of the electors of such village in the manner provided by sections four and five of title four of chapter two hundred ard ninety-one of the laws of eighteen hundred and seventy, and approved by the majority of the voters entitled to vote and voting on such question at an annual election or at a special election duly called.

§ 2. This act to take effect immediately.

INDEX TO REVISED CHARTER.

A

B

A

C

C

D

D

E

E

F

G

H

H

I

J

K

L

M

M

N

O

O

P

P

P

Q

R

S

S

T

T

T

U

V

W

W

CONTENTS OF APPENDIX.

LAWS AND ORDINANCES.

OF THE

VILLAGE OF GENEVA,

NEW YORK.

PUBLISHED BY AUTHORITY OF THE BOARD OF TRUSTEES.

COMPILED AND ARRANGED BY

GEORGE S. CONOVER

FOR THE BOARD OF TRUSTEES.

1891.

COURIER JOB PRINT.

In 1878 the Board of Trustees published a pamphlet containing the laws and ordinances of the village of Geneva, compiled and arranged by Geo. S. Conover, the then President of the village, in pursuance of the following action :

At a meeting of the Board of Trustees of the village of Geneva, held August 13th, 1878, the following preamble and resolution was adopted :

WHEREAS, the laws and ordinances of the Trustees of the village of Geneva, heretofore adopted and now in force, have been collated, codified and arranged by the President of this village, in appropriate chapters and sections, with suitable headings to each chapter, and by the said arrangement the laws and ordinances are rendered more plain, concise and intelligible, therefore

RESOLVED, That the codification and collation of the said laws and ordinances as re-arranged in chapters and sections, with the appropriate headings thereof, be and is hereby approved and adopted and the same be published in pamphlet form.

A true copy from the minutes.

W. H. SUYDAM,
Village Clerk.

To this publication was attached a certificate of W. H. Suydam, Village Clerk, attested with the village seal, certifying that they were a correct copy of the original, and were duly adopted at the times mentioned and had each been published once a week for two successive weeks in a village newspaper, and that "the same are now in force, and are published by authority of the Board of Trustees of the village of Geneva." This was dated tenth day of September, 1878.

In the year 1879 a supplemental sheet was issued containing some additional ordinances that had been adopted, to which was also attached a like certificate of W. H. Suydam, Village Clerk, dated 29th October, 1879.

The edition of the pamphlet having become exhausted and alterations and additions having been made at sundry times, in 1891 the Board of Trustees requested Geo. S. Conover to again compile and arrange the laws and ordinances of the village for publication. Having completed the duty assigned him, the compilation and arrangement was submitted to the Board of Trustees, who, after a thorough examination and careful consideration of the matter, took the following action.

At a regular meeting of the Board of Trustees of the village of Geneva, held June 16, 1891, it was

RESOLVED, That the codification and collation of the laws and ordinances as arranged in chapters and sections by Geo. S. Conover, under the direction of the Board of Trustees, be and the same is hereby approved and adopted, and ordered to be published in pamphlet form.

A true copy from the minutes.

HENRY B. GRAVES,
Village Clerk.

The undersigned would also hereby certify that the Laws and Ordinances of the Trustees of the village of Geneva, compiled and arranged by him, and published in this volume, were duly passed at the times stated, by the Board of Trustees, and that he has also a personal knowledge of the fact that the same were published in one of the newspapers published in the village of Geneva once in each week for two successive weeks, and that the same are now in force. GEO S. CONOVER.

Geneva, N. Y., June 25, 1891.

CONTENTS OF LAWS AND ORDINANCES.

LAWS AND ORDINANCES

OF THE

TRUSTEES OF THE VILLAGE OF GENEVA.

Adopted at the time specified at the head of each chapter except as otherwise stated at the end of the several sections.

CHAPTER I.

NUISANCES AND GOOD ORDER.

Adopted July 24, 1872.

The Trustees of the village of Geneva do enact the following Laws and Ordinances to be observed within the said village:

Penalty for permitting nuisance to remain on premises.

SECTION 1. Any person who shall suffer or permit any cellar, vault, private drain, pool, privy, sewer or grounds upon any premises belonging to or occupied by him, to become nuisances, foul, offensive or injurious to the public health, he or she shall be subject to a penalty of not less than five nor more than fifty dollars in every case; provided that the same has been declared to be a nuisance by the board of health, and notice to abate the same has been served on the person offending as aforesaid, by the clerk or other officer or member of the board. Such notice may be in writing or served personally. For every day the aforesaid nuisance shall continue after such notice, the person so continuing it shall be liable to a further penalty of three dollars.

Discharge or flow of foul substances upon sidewalks, streets.

§ 2. Any distiller, brewer, tanner, soap boiler, tallow chandler, livery stable keeper, or other person, who shall permit the discharge or overflow from any premises or grounds occupied by him or them, of any foul or nauseous liquor or substance of any kind whatever, into or upon any street, alley or sidewalk in the village, shall be subject to a penalty of not less than five nor more than fifty dollars for each and every such offense, and a like penalty for every twenty-four hours the same shall be continued after the first conviction, provided that the notice specified in the preceding section has been served upon the offending party.

Slaughter houses, petroleum refineries not allowed without permission of trustees.

§ 3. Any person who shall build, make or use, or cause to be built, made or used, any slaughter house, crude pretroleum refinery or place for the manufacture of any article made from crude petroleum, within the limits of the village, without the consent of the trustees first had and obtained, shall forfeit and pay the sum of twenty-five dollars, and a like sum for every day the same shall be used for said purposes, after notice to discontinue the same.

Penalty for depositing offensive substances in streets.

§ 4, Any person who shall throw, place or deposit, or permit any person in his or her employ to throw, place or deposit, any dung, dead animal, carrion, putrid meat or fish, entrails, shells of clams and oysters, decayed or decaying vegetables, or ashes, or nuisances of any kind, in or upon any sidewalk, street, alley, lane or park in the village, or shall cause or permit any such nuisance to be or remain in or upon any lot owned, used or occupied by him or her, shall pay a penalty of not less than five nor more than fifty dollars, and a like penalty for every twenty-four hours such nuisance shall remain after notice to abate the same.

Filth not to be allowed to run on to other premises or into streets.

§ 5. Any person who shall permit water, slops, or any kind of filth to run from his or her lot, or from a lot in his or her possession, onto any other lot or into any street, shall pay a penalty of not less than two nor more than fifteen dollars, and a like penalty for every twenty-four hours the same shall remain after notice to abate such nuisance.

§ 6. Any person who shall permit filth, slops or water to stand and remain upon any lot owned or occupied by him or her until the same becomes offensive or stagnant, shall pay a penalty of not less than three dollars, and a like penalty for every day the same shall remain after notice to abate such nuisance

Filth not to be permitted to remain upon lots.

§ 7. Whenever the owner or agent of any premises, in or upon which any nuisance may be found, are unknown or cannot be found, the board of health shall proceed to abate the same, and the expense of such abatement may be collected by suit against the owner, agent or occupant in the name of the trustees of the village of Geneva.

Board of health to abate nuisances on lots of unknown owners.

§ 8. Any person or persons who shall permit the discharge of, or overflow of water from the roof of any building, or from any eavetrough, conductor-pipe, awning, or anything attached to the front of any building, or from any waste pipe, or in any manner whatever, upon the sidewalk in front of any premises, shall be subject to and pay a penalty of not less than ten nor more than fifty dollars, and a further penalty of ten dollars for every twenty-four hours such nuisance, or the cause of such nuisance, shall remain after notice to abate or prevent the same.

Overflow of water on sidewalks.

Nothing in this section however shall prevent the extending of conductor pipes from the eavetrough of any building in a direct line and attached to the front of the building, to the sidewalk, provided a sufficient groove is made in said sidewalk from the building to the gutter, and in such a manner as shall be approved by the board of trustees of the village of Geneva. (Adopted March 5, 1878.)

Regulation for conductor pipes.

§ 9. No person or persons on or about any street, alley, lane, or other public place, shall make any indecent, immodest or immoral exhibition or exposure of his or her person, or cause or procure any other person to do so, or

Indecent exposure of person or indecent or profane language and nuisances.

make any indecent exposure of any animal or thing, or make use of any obscene, indecent or profane language, or commit any nuisance therein; any person who shall violate any or either of the provisions of this ordinance shall be liable to a penalty of not less than two dollars nor more than fifty dollars. (Adopted Dec. 8, 1874.)

Bathing within the limits.

§ 10. No person shall bathe in the waters of the Seneca lake, the canal, or Castle creek, after the rising of the sun and before eight o'clock in the evening, within the bounds of the corporation, under the penalty of not more than five dollars for each offense.

Procuring lewd women to remain.

§ 11. Any person who shall persuade, advise, or procure, or aid, countenance or assist in persuading, advising or procuring any lewd woman or women to come to, or to stop or remain within the village of Geneva, shall forfeit and pay a penalty of not more than fifty dollars.

Authorized to enter disorderly and houses of ill-fame, &c.

§ 12. The president of the village, police justice, or police constable, or persons summoned by them or any of them to aid them, may enter any disorderly house, house of ill-fame, house of prostitution or assignation, or gambling house or room, and arrest, with or without warrant, any suspicious persons found therein, and destroy any instruments or devices employed in gaming in such places, and, if admission be refused, may enter by force, by breaking the doors or otherwise.

Indecent exposure of stud horses in public places.

§ 13. Any person who shall indecently exhibit any stud horse, or let any such stud to mare within the village, unless in some enclosed place out of public view, shall pay a sum of not more than fifty dollars, on conviction, for each and every offense.

Abandoning sick animals.

§ 14. Any person who shall abandon or turn out at large within the bounds of the corporation, any old, lame or sick animal, shall pay a penalty of not less than five nor exceeding twenty-five dollars.

§ 15. All gunpowder which now is in or may hereafter be brought into the village, shall be deposited and kept in some powder magazine, to be kept at some point to be designated or approved by the board of trustees; and any person who shall keep or suffer to be kept in any building or place owned or occupied by him or her (except in such gunpowder magazine), a larger quantity of gunpowder than twelve and a half pounds for a longer period than three hours, shall forfeit and pay not less than ten nor more than fifty dollars for each offense; nor shall any person keep twelve and a half pounds as aforesaid or a less quantity, unless the same is securely kept in a tin canister with a tin cap or cover, and the same shall not be opened after candle light, under penalty of ten dollars for each offense.

Gunpowder to be kept at places approved by trustees.

§ 16. Any person who shall without permission of the trustees, prepare, discharge or let off any blast of gunpowder in the streets or elsewhere within the bounds of the village, or direct or procure such discharge, or be accessory thereto, shall pay a penalty of fifteen dollars for each and every such offense.

Blasting without permission.

§ 17. Any person who shall fire or discharge any cannon, gun, fowling-piece, pistol or fire arms of any description, or fire, explode, or set off any squib, cracker or other combustible or explosive material, without permission from the trustees, or written permission from the president of the village, shall pay a penalty of not more than ten dollars.

Firing guns, fireworks, &c.

Any person who shall violate any of the provisions of this section after the hour of eight o'clock in the evening, shall be subject to a penalty of not more than fifty dollars.

§ 18. Any person who shall immoderately drive or ride any horse or other animal in any avenue, street, alley or lane within the village, shall be liable to a penalty of not more than ten dollars.

Immoderate driving and riding.

Horse racing prohibited.

§ 19. There shall be no horse-racing within the bounds of the corporation, and any person who shall run any horse, or aid and abet such racing, shall, for every offense, pay a penalty of ten dollars.

Jumping on cars when under motion.

§ 20. No person, except a passenger or employee of the train, shall step or jump upon the step or platform of any car while the car is in motion, nor in any manner hang upon or to any step, platform, railing, bumper or coupling of any car or locomotive, while such car or locomotive is in motion, under a penalty of five dollars for each offense.

Ringing of gongs and bells

§ 21. No person shall ring any gong or bell in any street, lane or alley, or upon any sidewalk in the village of Geneva, under a penalty of not more than ten dollars for each offense. No tenant or occupant of any dwelling shall suffer any gong or bell to be rung as a call or signal upon any street, lane, alley or sidewalk in said village, under a penalty of not more than ten dollars for each offense.

Playing ball, flying kites—hand sleds.

§ 22. No person shall play ball,—beat, knock or drive any ball,—or raise or fly any kite in any public street, square or park in said village, or slide or ride down or upon any sidewalk upon any sled, sleigh or board, under a penalty of not more than ten dollars.

§ 23. * * * * *

Defacing or injuring lamp posts.

§ 24. Any person who shall climb upon or fasten a horse to any lamp post, or in any manner deface or injure the same, shall be subject to a penalty of not less than two nor more than ten dollars. (Adopted Dec. 8, 1874.)

Posting bills.

§ 25. No person shall paste, post, paint, print or nail upon any of the curb, gutter or flag stones, trees, lamp-posts, awning posts, horse posts, fences or buildings of this village, nor upon any public bridge, any handbill, poster, notice or advertisement, under a penalty of not less than two nor more than fifty dollars. (Adopted Dec. 8, 1874.)

§ 26. All persons who shall congregate in bodies or a crowd in or upon any street, lane, alley, park or other public place in this village, or upon any sidewalk, or cross-walk therein, for any purpose whatever to the annoyance or disturbance of citizens or travelers therein, and any person who shall obstruct or encumber any street corner or public place by standing or lounging in or about the same, shall be subject to a penalty of not less two nor more than ten dollars. (Adopted Dec. 8, 1874.)

Crowds in streets and sidewalks—lounging on corners, &c.

§ 27. Any person or persons who shall make or aid in making any disturbance or shall behave in a disorderly or indecent manner in any of the public halls, or other place of public amusement in this village, or in the entrances thereof, or who shall congregate in or hang around or about such entrance, or by lounging obstruct the free passage thereof at any time when the same shall be open for or during any concert, exhibition or other entertainment therein, shall be subject to and pay a penalty of not less than five dollars. (Adopted June 25, 1878.)

Public halls, disturbance in and around.

§ 28. Any person or persons who shall in any manner congregate or hang around or about the lock-up in the village of Geneva, or who shall make any noise or disturbance around or about the same, or who shall communicate or attempt to communicate with or annoy any person or persons confined therein, without the permission of the police justice or police constable of the village of Geneva, shall be guilty of an offense, and upon conviction pay a penalty of ten dollars. (Adopted June 25, 1878.)

Interference with lock-up.

§ 29. The proprietors of all saloons, shops and other places in which intoxicating liquors are sold, except taverns, inns, hotels and drug stores, within the corporate limits of the village of Geneva, shall close the same at twelve o'clock P. M., and keep the same closed until five o'clock the next morning; and the proprietors and keepers of all hotels, inns and taverns within the corporate limits of this village, shall close the bars or places where intoxi-

Hour of closing saloons and bars in hotels.

cating liquors are sold in their respective hotels, taverns or inns, at twelve o'clock P. M., and keep the same closed until five o'clock the next morning

Any person violating any of the provisions of this ordinance shall forfeit and pay a penalty of twenty-five dollars for each violation. (Adopted April 22, 1873. Amended January 22, 1884.)

Obstructions in Seneca lake.

§ 30. Any person who shall, in any manner, obstruc- the free navigation of the waters of the Seneca lake, within the bounds of the corporation, shall pay a penalty of ten dollars, and a further penalty of one dollar for every day such person shall permit such obstruction to remain, after receiving notice from any trustee or police constable to remove the same.

Obstructing officers in discharge of duty.

§ 31. Any person or persons who shall obstruct, or aid or assist in obstructing, any officer of the corporation in the execution of his duty, shall, for each and every offense, pay a penalty of not less than five dollars nor more than twenty-five dollars.

Hydrants, interference with, defacing or injuring.

§ 32. Any person who shall hitch or fasten a horse or any animal to any hydrant, or who shall climb upon, or post, paste, print or paint any handbill, poster, notice or advertisement, or shall in any manner deface or injure any hydrant, shall be subject to a penalty of not less than five nor more than fifty dollars. (Adopted May 22, 1877.)

Rail Roads, rate of speed.

§ 33. No railroad company nor any person shall direct, cause or suffer any engine, railroad car, or train of cars to be driven, drawn or propelled upon any railway within the village of Geneva at any greater speed than eight miles per hour, under a penalty of fifty dollars for each offense. (Adopted June 24, 1879.)

Steam whistles not to be sounded.

§ 34. No whistle connected with any railway engine, steamboat, steam-yacht or steam-tug shall be sounded or used within the corporate limits of the village of Geneva, except as a signal of immediate and impending danger, under a penalty of fifty dollars for each offense. (Adopted June 24, 1879.)

§ 35. Any person who shall be convicted of being an inmate of any house of ill-fame, or place for the practice of fornication, in the village of Geneva or shall be found loitering or strolling about the street in said village, by night, without regular lawful business, or who shall be convicted of being a prostitute, shall be subject to penalty in a sum of money of not less than ten nor more than fifty dollars for each and every offense. (Adopted August 18, 1885.) **Inmates of houses of ill-fame and street loiterers.**

§ 36. It shall not be lawful for any person to shoot with any target gun, air gun, pistol, filobert gun or pistol, or with any other gun or pistol, in or upon any street, alley, lane, park, or public place within the village of Geneva. **Shooting with guns and pistols prohibited.**

Any person who shall violate any provision of this section shall pay a penalty of not less than five dollars ($5) nor more than fifty dollars ($50). (Adopted August 25, 1885.)

CHAPTER II.

STREETS, PARKS, AND PUBLIC PLACES.

Adopted July 24, 1872.

The Trustees of the Village of Geneva do enact the following Laws and Ordinances to be observed within the said village:

SECTION 1. Any person who shall cut down, destroy or willfully break, mutilate or injure, or aid or assist in breaking, mutilating or injuring any fence, tree, shrubbery or fixtures now or hereafter erected, made, planted, set out or being in or upon any of the streets, places, parks or public squares in the village, or do any wilful damage thereto, shall pay a penalty of not less than five dollars for every such offense. **Injuring trees, shrubbery and flowers.**

Parks not to be used for bleaching, shaking carpets, or injured by horses cattle, &c.

§ 2. Any person who shall use any of the parks or public places within the village of Geneva as bleaching ground, or spread thereon any article of wearing apparel, cloth or clothes, or any goods whatever, or shake, beat, or cleanse any carpets, cloths or mats therein, or hang any clothing or other articles upon, or tie or fasten any horse or other animal to the fence surrounding the same, or lead or drive any team, horse, cattle, swine or other animal in or upon the same, or do any willful damage to any such parks or public places, shall pay a penalty of not less than three dollars nor more than twenty-five dollars for every violation of this ordinance. (Adopted June 30, 1874.)

Injuring grass in parks.

§ 3. Any person who shall cut down, pull up, or trample upon or injure the grass growing in any of the parks of the village, or stand or lie or walk upon any part of such parks, which is or may hereafter be laid out and appropriated for grass and shrubbery, shall pay a penalty of three dollars for each offense.

Killing birds or destroying their nests.

§ 4. Any person who shall climb, or throw stones or other material, or shoot into any tree in any park, public square, street or lane within this village, for the purpose of killing or frightening birds, or who shall attempt to carry off the young birds, or in any manner disturb the nest or nests of birds in any of the trees as aforesaid, shall pay a penalty of three dollars.

Shade trees, where to be planted; tying horses to.

§ 5. All shade trees hereafter to be set out, shall be within one foot of the outer line of the sidewalk. Any person violating this provision, or who shall neglect or refuse to move such trees when otherwise placed, on being required so to do by the street commissioner, shall forfeit and pay a penalty of five dollars for each offense. Any person who shall hitch any horse, mare or gelding, or other animal, to any tree so set within any sidewalk, shall forfeit and pay the sum of five dollars for each offense.

Shade trees to be trimmed up.

§ 6. All owners of lots or premises within this village shall keep all ornamental or shade trees, or shrubbery, standing within the line of the curb stone in front of such premises, or which shall project over any street or sidewalk in front of or adjoining such premises, so trimmed and cut that the lower limbs or branches thereof shall not be less than eight feet above such street or sidewalk, upon notice to that effect by the president, any trustee, or the police constable of the village.

Any person who shall fail to comply with this ordinance within twelve hours after such notice, shall pay a penalty of not less than two or more than five dollars, and an additional penalty of two dollars for every twenty-four hours' neglect or refusal so to comply.

Depositing rubbish in streets.

§ 7. Any person who shall throw or deposit (or cause the same to be done), ashes, dirt, stone, brick, straw, hay, grass, weeds, chips or rubbish, in any street, gutter, or any public square or park, except for the purpose of immediate removal, shall be subject to a penalty of not less than two dollars, and be liable, also, to pay all the expenses attending the removal of such rubbish or other things so deposited.

Building material in streets, president may grant permit for.

§ 8. The president may give permission in writing to any person to place and keep building material, to be used for the purpose of building, in any of the streets, alleys or public squares of the village in front of the lot or place where the building is proposed to be erected ; such permission shall not be for a longer period than three months, nor shall it authorize the obstruction of any of the sidewalks or gutters, nor more than one-half of the carriage way of the street opposite such lot or place. Any such permission may be revoked by the board of trustees.

Permit may be revoked.

Penalty for not removing within the time named in permit.

§ 9. Every person to whom permission is granted as aforesaid, shall cause all the timber, building materials and rubbish arising therefrom to be removed from the street by the expiration of the time named in the permit, under penalty of five dollars for every forty-eight hours the timber or materials aforesaid shall remain after the expiration of the time for which permission was given, but no single recovery shall exceed the sum of fifty dollars.

Building material not to be placed in streets.

§ 10. Any person who shall place or cause to be placed any stone, bricks, boards, planks, timber, lumber or other materials for building, in or upon any street, alley or public square in the village, without permission from the president or street commissioner, shall pay a penalty of five dollars for each offense, and the further penalty of three dollars for every twenty-four hours the same shall remain in such street, alley or public square, without such permission obtained in writing; any such permission may be revoked by the board of trustees whenever they shall deem proper, and every person obtaining such permission shall cause all such materials and the rubbish accumulated to be removed from the street, under penalty of five dollart for every twenty-four hours the same shall remain after the time named in the writing shall have terminated, or after notification of the revokement of the permit by the board of trustees.

Permit may be revoked.

Vehicles not to remain in streets.

§ 11. Any wagon maker, blacksmith, inn-keeper or other person who shall permit any wagon, carriage, cutter, sled, cart or other vehicle to remain in any public street or alley of this village detached from the animal or animals that respectively draw the same, shall pay a penalty of not less than five dollars for each offense; and if such wagon, cutter, sled, cart or other vehicle be so left or permitted to remain in any street or public alley of this village for six hours after written notice to the owner thereof, or the person so leaving or permitting the same to remain, to remove the same by the president or any trustee, police constable or street commissioner of this village, such wagon, carriage, cutter, sled, cart or other vehicle may be forthwith removed, by the president, any trustee, the street commissioner or his deputies, the police constable or any policeman, the expense of such removal to be paid by the owner of such vehicle; and all articles so taken to the pound shall be sold by the street commissioner for the expenses of such removal after five days' notice by public advertisement, unless such expenses shall have been previously paid. (Amended June 16, 1891.)

§ 12. Any person or persons who shall hereafter erect or cause to be erected any fence in front of his, her or their premises, which shall in any manner encroach upon the boundaries of any street in the village, shall be liable to a penalty of twenty-five dollars for every such offense; and every person whose fence or fences heretofore erected do now encroach upon the boundaries of any street, alley or public square, shall be liable in the penalty provided in this section, and upon refusing or neglecting to remove said fence or fences for six days after being notified by the street commissioner so to do, it shall be the duty of the street commissioner to remove the same, and the expenses thereof shall be added to the penalty aforesaid and paid into the village treasury.

Fences encroaching on streets to be removed.

§ 13. Any person who shall erect any building which shall project beyond the line of any street, and who, for twenty days after being notified by the street commissioner shall neglect or refuse to remove said building back to the line of the street, shall forfeit and pay the sum of twenty-five dollars, and a further sum of five dollars for every twenty-four hours said building shall remain beyond said time.

Buildings projecting beyond the line of street to be removed.

§ 14. Any person or persons who shall hereafter erect or cause to be erected any building or other fixture, or place any incumbrance in or upon any park, public square, street or alley within the boundaries of the village, shall be liable to a penalty in the sum of twenty-five dollars for every such offense, and to a further penalty of ten dollars for every twenty-four hours such building, fixture or incumbrance shall remain in or upon such public square, street, alley or park, after notice of removal shall have been given by the street commissioner, village clerk, or other officer authorized by the board of trustees to give such notice; and any person or persons whose building, fixture or incumbrance does now remain in or upon any park, public square, street or alley, and who shall neglect or refuse to remove the same within the time specified in the notice

Buildings or obstructions in streets, &c.

requiring its removal, shall be liable in the penalty provided in this section, and also in the further penalty provided in this section for every twenty-four hours such building, fixture or incumbrance shall remain in or upon any park, public square, street or alley after the notice is given as herein provided; and on the expiration of the time given in said notice for removal, the street commissioner shall have power to remove or cause to be removed any building, fixture or incumbrance now erected or placed, or hereafter erected or placed upon any park, public square, street or alley, and the owner of said building, fixture or incumbrance shall be liable to pay the expense of such removal in addition to the penalty aforesaid. Said notice may be served personally, or by leaving a written or partly written and partly printed notice at the residence or usual place of business of the owner of such building, fixture or incumbrance; or if he or she be a non-resident, a notice deposited in the post office directed to his or her last known place of residence shall be deemed sufficient.

Notice how served.

Cross-walks to be kept free from obstructions.

§ 15. All cross-walks within the village shall be kept and reserved from any sleighs, wagons, carts or other vehicles being placed thereon, except so far as may be necessary in passing and repassing the same without continuing thereon any longer, and the owner or driver of any sleigh, wagon or other vehicle, offending against the provisions of this section, shall pay a penalty of five dollars.

Horses not to be left in streets without being securely tied.

§ 16. Any person who shall leave any horse or horses in the street without the same being sufficiently tied, shall be liable to a penalty of three dollars; and any person who shall hitch or fasten a horse or other animal to any lamp post, or to any tree, or shall climb, whittle, bruise or otherwise injure any tree in any street, public square or park, shall pay a penalty of not more than fifteen dollars.

Vehicles not to remain on bridges.

§ 17. Any owner or driver of any cart, sleigh, sled, wagon or other vehicle, who shall suffer such vehicle to remain on any bridge in the village for any time longer than is necessary to pass over the same, shall pay a penalty of five dollars for each offense.

Sidewalks, repairs of.

§ 18. Whenever any sidewalk in front of any premises shall, in the judgment of the board of trustees, require repairs, the street commissioner or the village clerk shall notify the owner or agent of such property that he or she must repair said walk as required by the charter.

Sidewalks to be kept free from obstructions.

§ 19. The occupant of each and every house, tenement and building in said village, fronting or being upon any street or streets, the sidewalks or walks of which are of plank, stone or brick—or the owner, occupant or agent of any vacant lot fronting or being as aforesaid—shall keep such sidewalk or walks clean and free from obstructions, shall clear the same of snow and ice by ten o'clock in the forenoon of each day, and cause the same to be kept clear from snow and ice for the space of twenty-four hours after the snow has fallen or the ice accumulated, under a penalty of not less than two dollars for any and every neglect or refusal so to do If, however, the snow and ice cannot at any time be effectually removed as is by this section required, then the person or persons aforesaid shall sufficiently cover such walks with sand or ashes so that traveling thereon shall not be perilous; under a penalty of not less than two dollars for every such neglect. If the snow and ice be not cleaned off in the manner above indicated, then the president, any trustee, or the street commissioner may cause the same to be removed, and commence suit for the penalty, which in such case shall not be less than the expense of such removal together with costs of suit. That such penalty when collected, or so much thereof as may be necessary for that purpose, shall be applied to the payment of the expense aforesaid.

Snow and ice to be removed from. *Or covered with sand or ashes.* *Penalty.*

Slush and mud.

The provisions of this section so far as they shall be applicable shall apply to slush and mud under the like penalties. (Adopted Dec. 8, 1874.)

Sidewalks and cross-walks not to be obstructed by horses, vehicles, or auction crowds.

§ 20. Any person who shall fasten a horse in such a way that the vehicle, reins or lines shall be an obstacle to the free use of any sidewalk or crosswalk, shall forfeit and pay the sum of five dollars; and if any person shall lead, push, draw or suffer to remain upon any sidewalk, any horse or any vehicle, he or she shall pay a penalty of five dollars for each offense; any person who shall sell or attempt to sell or cry for sale at auction any goods, chattels or personal property, upon any sidewalk, so as to collect a crowd of people, whereby the free passage is prevented or hindered to persons wishing to pass along said sidewalk, shall be subject to a penalty of five dollars; any person who shall saw or split wood upon any sidewalk shall be subject to a penalty of five dollars for each offense; any person who shall curry or clean any horse, or wash, clean or grease any wagon, carriage or other vehicle on any sidewalk, or encumber the same with any vehicle, shall pay a penalty of five dollars for every such offense.

Wood not to be piled or split.

Horses not to be cleaned or wagons washed or greased on.

Auctions and sales in streets.

§ 21. No person shall sell or offer or expose for sale, at public auction or outcry, upon any of the streets, alleys, sidewalks or public grounds of the village, any goods, wares, merchandise, furniture, or other articles whatsoever, or any horse or other animal, without the written permit of the president, and also of the owner of the premises in front of which the sale shall take place; nor shall any person sell, or offer or expose for sale in any street, alley, sidewalk, or public ground any article of merchandise, without a written permit from the president, except persons attending public markets, and selling in accordance with the regulations thereof, under a penalty of not more than fifty dollars.

Sidewalks and cross-walks, mortar not to be mixed on.

§ 22. Any person who shall mix or temper mortar upon any sidewalk or any crosswalk in the village, shall forfeit and pay a penalty of five dollars for each offense; any person who shall draw or shove, or cause the same to

Wheelbarrows,

done, any wheelbarrow, hand-cart or hand-wagon used for

the conveyance of baggage, or any articles of property, upon any sidewalk, (except to cross the same), shall be liable to a penalty of two dollars for each offense; any person who shall place any cask, box, plank, board or other articles on any sidewalk, shall pay a penalty therefor of not less than one nor more than five dollars; and any cask, box, barrel, plank, board or other articles left on any sidewalk for six hours after written notice to the party owning or permitting the same to so remain by the president, any trustee or street commissioner of this village, may be reremoved by the president, any trustee, the street commissioner or his deputies, the police constable or any policeman, and such articles shall be sold for the expenses of such removal by the street commissioner after five days' notice by public advertisement, unless such expense of removal shall have been previously paid; but nothing herein contained shall prohibit merchants and others from placing goods and merchandise and furniture on the sidewalk for the purpose of loading and unloading the same without unreasonable delay.

hand-carts, boxes and other obstructions on.

Articles may be taken and removed.

§ 23. Any person who shall erect or cause to be erected, any stairs leading from the sidewalk and continuing over the same, to an entrance in the first or second story of any building, shall first get the permission of the board of trustees and the approval of the president therefor, under penalty of five dollars, and pay the further penalty of three dollars for every twenty-four hours the stairs shall remain after notice served to remove the same by any officer of the village.

Stairs not to be erected from sidewalks without permission of trustees.

§ 24. Any person who shall fix, put up, erect or suffer to remain fixed, put up, or erected, any sign, post or fixture, projecting into or over any sidewalk or street more than three feet, shall pay a penalty of ten dollars, and the further sum of two dollars for every forty-eight hours the same shall remain after being notified to remove the same by the president, any trustee, or police constable.

Posts or projecting signs over sidewalks.

Awnings, wooden.

§ 25. No person or persons shall hereafter erect any wooden awning upon or over any of the sidewalks of this village, under a penalty of twenty-five dollars, and a further penalty of two dollars for every twenty-four hours such awning shall remain after notice to take the same down has been given by the president, any trustee, street commissioner, or police constable.

Cloth or other.

Nor shall any cloth or other awning be hereafter erected, unless it shall be at least seven feet elevation from and not extend more than six feet over the walk, under a penalty of five dollars, and a further penalty of one dollar for every twenty-four hours it shall remain after notice to remove the same as in the case of wooden awnings.

Goods not to be suspended.

Nor shall any goods, wares or merchandise be suspended or placed in front of any store, shop or other building, which shall extend more than six feet over the walk, or higher therefrom than four feet, under a penalty of five dollars; but goods, wares and merchandise may be suspended against the wall of any store or other building, provided they do not project from the building further than fourteen inches.

Horses, not to drive on sidewalks.

§ 26. Any person who shall drive or lead any team, horse or other animal on to or across any sidewalk in this village, shall pay a penalty of not less than two nor more than ten dollars; but nothing herein contained shall prevent the owners or occupants of lots from driving across the lots in front of their premises, where a driveway has been properly constructed for that purpose. (Adopted Dec. 7, 1884.)

Streets and sidewalks not to be dug up without permission in writing.

§ 27. No person shall injure or tear up any pavement or street cross-walk, or sidewalk, nor shall any person dig any hole or trench in any street, to connect with a sewer, water or gas pipe, or for any other purpose, without first obtaining the consent of the board of trustees, or the permission of the president in writing. Any person violating the foregoing provisions of this ordinance shall be subject to a penalty of not less than five nor more than fifty dollars. When consent or permission shall be obtained to connect with a sewer, the person obtaining the same or making such connection, or his guarantees, shall not be entitled to claim of the village any damages sustained by reason of the flooding of the sewer with which such connection shall be made, whether such flooding shall be occasioned by want of capacity or obstruction therein; and any person who shall connect a drain or sewer from their premises with any public sewer, shall waive all damages which they may be subjected to on account of backwater from such public sewer; and each and every person who shall dig in any street as aforesaid shall do the same with due diligence, and replace any sidewalk, crosswalk or pavement that may have been displaced on account thereof in a good and substantial manner, and to lay the same in fine gravel or sand; and where such hole or trench shall be made, the dirt and gravel therefrom shall be kept separately, and in refilling such hole or trench the dirt shall be put in the bottom thereof and thoroughly pounded down, and the gravel replaced on the top. Such person or persons shall cause a proper grade to be restored where such hole or trench shall have been made and maintain the same for one year thereafter; under a penalty of not less than five nor more than fifty dollars. (Adopted Dec. 8, 1874.)

Connecting with sewer.

Excavations to be made with due diligence and substantially refilled.

Grade to be restored and maintained.

§ 28. Whenever the "president, directors and company" of the "Geneva Water Works," or "the Geneva Gas Light Company," shall tear up any pavement or cross-walk, or dig in any street, lane or alley of said village, for the purpose of laying, repairing or changing any of their pipes or conduits, in pursuance of their respective charters, the same shall be done with due diligence, and said pavement and cross-walks replaced in a good and substantial manner, and to be relaid in fine gravel or sand; that such street, lane or alley, where such digging may be done, shall be

Gas and water works companies digging in streets.

refilled with earth, thoroughly pounded down, and properly leveled and graded, and the grade thereof maintained by them for a year then next ensuing. Any violation of the foregoing provisions of this section shall be subjected to a penalty of not less than five nor more than fifty dollars. The president, any trustee, or the street commissioner, may cause the aforesaid repairs to be made in accordance with said provisions, and commence suit for the penalty, which in such case shall not be less than the expense of such repairs together with the costs of suit. That such penalty when collected, or so much thereof as may be necessary, shall be applied to the payment of the expense aforesaid. (Adopted Dec. 8, 1874.)

Penalty for altering grade of streets, &c.

§ 29. Any person who shall place, deposit or cause to be placed or deposited any earth, gravel, sand, ashes, stone or any other material for the purpose of filling up, or altering the grade of any street, gutter, sidewalk, park or public grounds of this village, or who shall deposit or cause to be deposited any such material in said places for any other purpose except for immediate removal; or who shall make or cause to be made any excavation for the like or any other purpose: or who shall alter or do anything that may tend to alter any such grade without the consent of the board of trustees, shall be subject to a penalty of twenty-five dollars and a further penalty of ten dollars for every day any such material shall remain, or any such excavation is not properly filled up, or any alteration of such grade shall remain after notice to restore such grade, remove such material or properly refill such excavation shall have been given by the president of the village, the street commissioner or any person authorized by them or either of them, or by the order of the board of trustees, which notice may be served personally or by leaving a copy of the same at the residence or usual place of business of the party offending. (Adopted Aug. 21, 1877.)

Grade of streets to be maintained.

§ 30. It shall be the duty of the president of the village, or the street commissioner, and they or either of them are hereby authorized to cause the grade of any street, gutter, sidewalk, park or other public place to be restored, maintained, kept up and sustained, and to do or cause to be done any work, or labor to be performed to restore such grade, and the expense thereof shall be paid by the party offending, and to be a lien on the premises of any such party, such expense to be in addition to the penalty prescribed in the preceding section ; and the president or street commissioner is hereby authorized and empowered, and it shall be their duty to resist any attempt that shall be made to alter any such grade, and any interferance with them or either of them, or with any person authorized by the board of trustees, or with any workmen under the direction of the aforesaid, or in the employ of the village at such times, or any other time, shall subject the offender to a penalty of twenty-five dollars. (Adopted Aug. 21, 1877.)

Interference with workmen.

§ 31. Any person who shall, without written permission from the president, dig, remove or carry away, or cause the same to be done, any stone, earth, sand or gravel from any street, highway, lane or public square in the village, shall pay a penalty of five dollars for each offense.

Earth not to be removed from streets without permission.

§ 32. Any person who shall place or suffer to be placed or to remain in or upon any of the streets or sidewalks of this village any obstruction, or shall break, disturb, excavate or trench in or upon any street or sidewalk, for the purpose of laying or repairing any pavement, water pipe, drain or gas pipe, or for any other purpose, shall keep one or more lanterns burning in a conspicuous place to indicate such obstacle, trench or breach, during the nights the same shall remain such; and shall also build and place about any trench or opening made in any street or sidewalk a temporary fence or railing sufficiently high and secure to prevent persons, cattle or horses falling into the same. All persons violating any of the provisions of this section shall be liable to a penalty of not more than twenty nor less than five dollars for each offense.

Lighted lanterns over obstructions in streets at night.

Fences to be placed around excavations.

Streets not to be obstructed or occupied contrary to law.

§ 33. Every person who shall obstruct, occupy or use any part of any street, walk, alley, public square or other public grounds, in any manner or for any other purpose than is authorized by law or expressly permitted by the ordinances of this village, shall for each and every offense pay a penalty of ten dollars.

Railroad cars obstructing streets.

§ 34. Any person or corporation owning or having control or management of any railroad tracks or cars, that shall leave upon any railroad track or switch track where the same crosses or occupies any portion of any street or alley of this village, any car or cars detached from a locomotive, or any person who shall have control of such cars so placed for the purpose of loading with freight, shall be subject to a penalty of ten dollars for each violation of this ordinance, and to a further penalty of ten dollars for every twenty-four hours such car or cars shall be so left after notice from the street commissioner or village clerk to remove the same. (Adopted June 25, 1878.

Washing wagons in streets on line of water works.

§ 35. Any person or persons who shall wash or cause to be washed any carriage or other vehicle in or upon any street of this village through which water pipes are laid, shall be subject to a penalty of five dollars for each violation of this ordinance. (Adopted June 25, 1878.)

Auctioneers to be licensed.

§ 36. Any auctioneer, or other person, who shall expose or offer for sale, at auction, any goods, wares or merchandise, of any name or nature whatsoever, in any building, or upon any of the public squares, streets or alleys in the village of Geneva, shall first obtain a license therefor from the president of the board of trustees of said village, for which he or she shall be charged not less than five dollars nor more than twenty-five dollars for one day, the amount between said limits to be at the discretion of the President of the village or of the board of trustees of the village of Geneva, when referred to them.

And, any person who shall violate any of the provisions of this section shall pay a penalty of not less than ten nor more than fifty dollars, and the further sum of fifteen dollars for every day he or she may continue the same.

Licenses shall be granted as aforesaid upon application therefor, and payment of the license fee to be fixed in each particular case as herein before limited by the president of the village, or by the board of trustees of the village, on appeal thereto.

The license shall specify the object and length of time for which the same is paid. Adopted Dec. 19, 1882.)

§ 37. Any person or persons who shall distribute by throwing or placing on the sidewalks, streets, steps or any public square or place or conveyances standing thereon (or cause the same to be done) any advertising bill, paper, circular or other substance, thereby littering up said sidewalks, streets, etc., shall be liable to pay a penalty of not less than five nor more than ten dollars. (Adopted Dec. 27, 1881.)

Handbills, &c., not to be thrown in streets or wagons.

§ 38. No private connection shall hereafter be made with any public sewer in this village, except under supervision of the street commissioner or some other person designated or appointed by the board of trustees, or the president of the village, upon a written *application* made therefor. Any person violating the provisions of this ordinance shall be subject to a penalty of not less than five nor more than fifty dollars. (Adopted June 16, 1891.)*

Sewer openings, how permitted.

§ 39. No deed of any new street shall be accepted by the board of trustees unless accompanied by a map made by a competent surveyor and stone monuments with exact points to mark the boundaries be set, and provided also that no street shall hereafter be accepted nor any expendi-

New streets not to be accepted unless monumented and map filed.

---

*At a meeting of the board of trustees, held June 30, 1891, the following resolution was adopted:

Resolved, That the foregoing ordinance be published in its proper place in the pamphlet containing the laws and ordinances of this village, already ordered to be published.

ture made thereon unless the same has been previously properly graded. (Adopted June 30, 1891.)

Handbills, fruit peeling, dust, garbage, ashes and litter not to put in streets or sidewalks.

§ 40. Any person who shall sweep, throw or deposit upon any of the sidewalks within the village of Geneva, or upon any of the streets thereof, any dust, ashes, garbage, fruit or fruit peeling, hand-bills, circulars or other paper, shall be subject to a penalty of not less than two dollars and be liable also to pay all expenses attending the removal of said rubbish or other things so deposited. (Adopted June 16, 1891.

CHAPTER III.

FIRES AND FIRE DEPARTMENT

Adopted July 24, 1872.

The Trustees of the Village of Geneva do enact the following Laws and Ordinances to be observed within the said Village:

Engineer to have charge of apparatus.

SECTION 1. The chief engineer and assistant engineers shall have full control of the firemen at all fires, to order and direct in the management of their engines, hooks and ladders, hose and all other apparatus.

Annual report to board of trustees.

§ 2. The chief engineer shall report annually to the board of trustees, and at such other times as may be required, the condition of the engines, hooks and ladders, hose and house for the keeping of the same, and all other fire apparatus, and recommend such alterations and improvements in the same as he may think proper, and also report the names of such firemen as have disobeyed orders or neglected or refused to attend to their duty. Whenever

Repairs to engines be made.

the engines or other fire apparatus shall want repairs, he shall, with the committee on fire department, cause the same to be done immediately, provided the expense thereof shall not exceed twenty dollars, and report to the village clerk at the expiration of every month the amount of expenditures so made or ordered. Any repairs that may be needed to any fire department building or apparatus involving a larger expenditure than twenty dollars, the chief engineer shall report the same, with the kind of repairs required, to the board of trustees. not exceeding twenty dollars.

§ 3. The firemen shall be divided into companies, to consist of such persons as the board of trustees shall from time to time direct, to take charge of, under the direction of the chief engineer, the fire engines, hose, hooks and ladders, and such other fire apparatus as may be placed in their charge belonging to the village of Geneva. To have charge of apparatus.

§ 4. The different fire companies shall be under the control of and subject to the direction of the chief engineer and assistant engineers, and upon any alarm of fire the said companies shall immediately repair to the place of the fire with the engines, hose, hooks and ladders, and other implements in their charge, and there work and manage the same under the direction of the chief engineer and his assistants, and in case of their absence place and work their fire apparatus in the most effectual manner until the fire shall be extinguished, and shall not remove therefrom but by permission of the chief engineer, or, in his absence, an assistant engineer, and on such permission they shall return their respective engines, hooks and ladders, and hook and ladder carriages to their respective places of deposit, and cause the same to be well washed and cleansed within twenty-four hours; and whenever the chief engineer shall find that the apparatus in the possession of any company has not been properly washed and cleansed within the time herein mentioned, after it has been used for any purpose, he is authorized to cause the same to be cleansed, and deduct the expense thereof from any money then due or that may thereafter become due the company for whom such work was done. Duty of firemen at fires.

Repairs to engines and apparatus, how to be made.

§ 5. The foreman having charge of any engine or other apparatus shall have the same kept in good order for immediate use; he shall report immediately to the chief engineer when any repairs are needed to the same or to the building in which they are contained, and the foreman and all other officers or officer, or members or member of any engine, hook and ladder or hose company, are hereby forbid having any repairs done to any apparatus in their charge or to the building in which they are kept, under penalty of ten dollars; and the trustees hereby refuse to pay any bills that may be contracted in violation of this section. The foreman or any officer or member of any fire company, or any other person or persons, are hereby forbid making any alteration or addition to any engine or other fire apparatus belonging to the village, which shall increase or decrease its capacity, without the permission of the chief engineer, under penalty of twenty-five dollars for each and every offense.

Permission of chief engineer to be had for using engines.

§ 6. If any person or company, having charge of any engine, hose or other fire apparatus belonging to the village of Geneva, shall suffer or permit the same to be applied to private use without the written consent of the chief engineer, or in his absence from the village, the acting chief engineer, he shall forfeit the penalty of ten dollars for each and every such offense, besides being liable for all damages. No person or persons shall, without the written permission of the water works company and the president of the village, take water, except for the extinguishment of fires, from any village hydrant, reservoir or cistern, under penalty of ten dollars for each and every offense, besides being liable for all damages.

Water from hydrants or cisterns not to be used without permit.

Not to run on sidewalks with machine.

§ 7. No fire engine, hook, ladder, hose carriage or hose cart shall, in going to or returning from any fire or alarm of fire, or at any other time, be run, drawn, wheeled or driven on any sidewalk, under the penalty of ten dollars for each offense, to be forfeited by any company violating the provisions of this ordinance; nor shall they in returning from a fire or alarm of fire, be drawn faster than a walk, under a penalty of ten dollars.

Companies to adopt such by-laws as board of trustees may approve.

§ 8. Each engine, hook and ladder or hose company not attached to any engine company, respectively may adopt such constitution and by-laws and regulations for their government, subordinate to the ordinanees of the village, as they may deem best calculated to accomplish the objects for which the respective companies were organized, and present the same to the board of trustees for their approval.

Members may be sued for company dues.

§ 9. Whenever any member of the fire department shall be justly indebted to said company, in pursuance of the constitution, by-laws or regulations of the same, (they having first been submitted to and approved by the board of trustees,) it shall be lawful for said company to sue for and recover from such member, on his neglect or refusal to pay whatever sum may be so due, by action for debt or otherwise, in the name of the corporation, for the use of said company, before any court having jurisdiction.

Persons to obey officers at fires.

§ 10. Any person who may repair to a fire shall be obedient to the orders of the president, any trustee, police constable, any policeman, chief or assistant engineer, or acting foreman of any fire company, in working on any engine or assisting in drawing any fire apparatus to the fire and in removing or protecting any property; and in case any person shall refuse to obey such orders, he shall be liable to a penalty of five dollars.

President and chief engineer may grant leave of absence.

§ 11. The president and chief engineer shall have power, in their discretion, to grant permission to any fire company to go with their respective engines or fire apparatus beyond the limits of the village, to be absent such length of time as they may direct. Any officer in command of any company, who shall suffer or permit any engine or other apparatus in r chage of any company, to be taken beyond the village limits without such permission, shall forfeit and pay for every such offense a penalty of twenty-five dollars, besides being liable for all damages.

Not to injure apparatus.

§ 12. If any person shall enter any engine, hose or hook and ladder house in this village in order to do any injury thereto or to any of the apparatus for extinguishing fires, or shall injure or mutilate, at any time or place, any of the apparatus for extinguishing fires, or any of the public cisterns, hydrants or fire stops now constructed or to be constructed, or shall draw any water therefrom for any other purpose than for the use of the engines, without written permission from the water works company and the president of the village, such person shall be liable to a penalty not exceeding twenty-five dollars over and above private damages that may be sustained. But nothing herein contained shall be construed to prohibit the president, any trustee, or chief engineer and assistants from the use of water at any time for the purpose of testing the condition of the hydrants, cisterns and fire apparatus.

Not to draw water from hydrants or cisterns.

Exception.

False alarm of fire.

§ 13. Any person who shall knowingly raise a false alarm of fire shall pay a penalty of not less than five nor more than fifty dollars. (Adopted Sep. 6, 1886.)

Protection of property at fires.

§ 14. It shall be the duty of the police constable and fire-wardens to repair to and attend every fire; to protect and preserve property, and to prevent the same from being carried away unless by the authority of the owner.

Mutinous conduct at fires.

§ 15. Any person who shall at the time of any fire be guilty of mutinous conduct, or attempt to excite insubordination in others, or obstruct the operations of the fire department, or the execution of the orders of the proper officers, or shall at any time or place maliciously injure, in any manner, any fire apparatus belonging to the corporation, shall forfeit and pay a penalty not less than twenty-five dollars nor exceeding fifty dollars, besides being liable to action in law for the recovery of any damage by the violation of any part of this ordinance; and if the person so offending shall be a fireman, he shall, on conviction, be removed.

§ 16. No person shall ride or drive any sleigh, carriage, cart, wagon or other vehicle upon or across any hose used by the fire department of the village of Geneva, in any street, lane, alley or other place in said village, under a penalty of twenty dollars for each and every offense. (Adopted April 2, 1878.) Hose not to be driven over.

CHAPTER IV.

PREVENTION OF FIRES.

Adopted July 24, 1872.

The Trustees of the Village of Geneva do enact the following Laws and Ordinances to be observed within the said Village:

SECTION 1. The pipe of any stove, franklin or boiler, that is now or may hereafter be put up, shall be conducted into a chimney made of brick or stone, except in cases where the chief engineer of the fire department shall deem it equally safe if otherwise put up, to be certified under his hand. All cooper shops and other places used for manufacturing purposes, shall have constructed a sufficient chimney made of brick or stone. Any person violating any of the provisions of this section shall forfeit five dollars for every offense, and a further sum of two dollars for every twenty-four hours such violation shall continue after such person shall have been notified by the fire wardens to comply with the provisions of this section, Stove pipes. Cooper shops and manufactories.

§ 2. No person shall keep or deposit within the bounds of the corporation any ashes, unless the same are kept or deposited in a secure earthen, metal, or other incombustible enclosure, or upon the ground separate and apart from all combustible matter, under the penalty of one dollar for each offense. Ashes how to be deposited.

Unslacked lime.

§ 3. No unslacked lime shall be deposited within twenty feet of any building, without permission from a trustee or street commissioner. Any person violating this ordinance shall pay a penalty of five dollars.

Illuminating oil to be tested.

§ 4. No person shall keep, store, or sell or expose for sale any illuminating oil or fluid, standing under the fire test of one hundred and ten degrees, under the penalty of ten dollars for each offense.

Explosive materials not to be sold at night

§ 5. No person shall, in the evening, by candle or other light, weigh or sell gunpowder or gun-cotton in bulk, or draw, measure, or sell any gasoline, benzine, or naptha, under a penalty of twenty-five dollars for each offense.

Fire wardens, their duties.

§ 6. It shall be the duty of the fire wardens, and they are hereby authorized to examine all houses, stores, yards and outbuildings, to ascertain if they are in a dangerous state in regard to fires: and it shall further be their duty to notify and require the owner or occupant of any premises which they may find in a condition likely, in their opinion, to produce danger from fire, to put the same in a safe and seecure condition; also to make a report in writing of their doings at the next stated meeting of the board of trustees after each visitation. (Adopted April 22, 1873.)

§ 7. No person or persons shall, within the fire limits in this village, keep, deposit or store at any one time, in any building, shed or place contiguous thereto, any kerosene oil, crude petroleum, or combustible products thereof, in greater quantities than five barrels; said oil to be kept in some secure place, free from danger of fire—to be approvof by the fire wardens—under a penalty of not less than fifteen nor more than fifty dollars. (Adopted September 30, 1879.)

CHAPTER V.

HACKS, CARRIAGES, PORTERS, RUNNERS, &C.

Adopted July 24, 1872.

The Trustees of the Village of Geneva do enact the following Laws and Ordinances to be observed within the said village.

SECTION 1. Any person keeping, or who may keep a hackney coach, cab or other carriage or wagon for hire, for the conveyance of passengers or baggage within the bounds of said village, shall cause such hackney coach, cab, carriage or wagon to be numbered, and such number to be not less than two by three inches in size, and to be placed on both sides of said vehicle, and to be approved by the village clerk, and file the same with said clerk with the name and place of residence of such owner or keeper. All persons violating any of the provisions of this section shall be liable to a penalty of not more than ten dollars. (Adopted April 23, 1873.) **Hacks, carriages, &c., to be numbered.**

§ 2. Any person keeping or who may keep a hackney coach, cab or other carriage or wagon for hire, for the conveyance of passengers or baggage within the bounds of the village, shall obtain from the president a license therefor, and such license, stating the number of the coach, cab or carriage, shall continue in force until the fifteenth day of April after the date thereof, and any person keeping any hackney coach, cab or other carriage for hire in such village without such license, shall be liable to a penalty in the sum of ten dollars for each offense. **To be licensed.**

§ 3. Any person procuring such license shall pay therefor the sum of three dollars if two horses be attached, and two dollars if for one horse only. **License fees.**

§ 4. The board of trustees are hereby authorized to make, from time to time, such regulations respecting the stands for hacks, cabs or other carriages as may in **Where to stand** their judgment seem to be necessary to preserve order and promote the public convenience; and any person refusing to comply with their directions or regulations shall, for every offense, pay a penalty of five dollars.

Runners not to solicit without license.

§ 5. Any person who shall, without license, within the corporate bounds of the village, solicit passengers or others, or their baggage, for any hack, cab, or other carriage, shall incur the penalty of ten dollars for each and every such offense, provided that the keepers of livery stables shall have the right to do the ordinary and legitimate business of such stable without obtaining license therefor.

Proprietors and runners to have license, wear badges, &c.

§ 6. Any person of good moral character, on application to the president in writing, shall be entitled to a license to act as "public porter and runner," upon the payment of the sum of three dollars, Every person so licensed shall wear a badge with his name and the number of his license plainly painted or engraved thereon, visible at all times to the persons employing him, under penalty of three dollars for each offense.

Porters of hotels may have porter's license changed.

§ 7. The keeper or keepers of any public house or hotel, who shall have obtained a license for any porter in his, her or their employ, may have the same revoked and be entitled to another for the remaining portion of the year without additional fee therefor; provided, that no such license shall be changed or transferred to any other hotel or public house without an order from the president; and each and every keeper of such hotel or public house shall be personally liable for each and every violation of the ordinances in reference to "public porters and runners," when committed by any porter or runner in his, her or their employ, or who shall be acting under the license granted to any such hotel or public house keeper.

Penalty for acting as porter or runner without license.

§ 8. Any person who shall, without a license, act as public porter or runner, either for himself or for any hotel, public house, steamboat, railroad, canal boat or other transportation line, or ask the custom or patronage of any traveler or other person, shall be liable to a penalty therefor of not less than three dollars.

§ 9. Any porter or runner who shall, at any railroad depot, station, steamboat landing, or at any other place, make use of device, deceit, imposition, or false representation in relation to the charge of fare, character, custom or location of any public house, hotel or private house, or street, place of business, locality or number whatever in said village, or in relation to the time or place of the arrival or departure of any boat, stage, omnibus or railroad car or train, or other conveyance, to any stranger, nonresident or citizen, shall be subject to a penalty of not less than five dollars; and any porter or runner who shall, at any time or place, when engaged in his employment, or at any time in any railroad depot, station or steamboat landing, make use of any language, or commit any act calculated to disturb the public peace or the good order of the place, or vex or disturb strangers or citizens, shall be subject to a penalty of not less than five dollars nor more than fifty dollars.

Porters and runners not to misrepresent.

Not to make use of boisterous language.

§ 10. All licenses granted under these ordinances shall expire or be renewed on the fifteenth day of April in each year; and any person who shall violate any section, clause or provision of the ordinances relating to porters or runners or shall fail to perform any act or thing required thereby, shall pay a penalty of not less than three nor more than fifty dollars, and if committed by any such licensed porter or runner herein provided for, his license may be revoked on the second offense at the discretion of the board of trustees.

License to expire 15th April in each year.

§ 11. Any license granted pursuant to the provisions of this chapter, may be revoked by the president on complaint made and an investigation of the case by him, if in his discretion he shall think proper.

President may revoke license.

CHAPTER VI.

CARTS.

Adopted July 24, 1872.

The Trustees of the village of Geneva do enact the following Laws and Ordinances to be observed within the said village:

Cartmen to be licensed.

SECTION 1. No person shall within the village of Geneva pursue the business of a cartman without having a license from the trustees for that purpose, and in all other respects complying with ordinances of the board of trustees of said village in relation to that subject, under a penalty of three dollars for each offense.

Carts to be numbered.

§ 2. Every cartman shall cause his cart to be numbered, and such number to be approved by the village clerk, and file the same with said clerk, with the name and place of residence of such cartman.

Where cart may stand.

§ 3. The board of trustees are hereby authorized to make, from time to time, such regulations respecting the stands for trucks or wagons while waiting for employment, as in their judgment may best promote the public convenience; and no cart, truck or wagon shall be permitted by the owner or driver thereof to stand waiting for employment in any other public street or place in the village than as so designated; and any person or persons refusing to comply with the regulations so made, shall for every offense forfeit the sum of three dollars.

CHAPTER VII.

CEMETERIES.

Adopted July 24, 1872.

The Trustees of the village of Geneva do enact the following Laws and Ordinances to be observed within the said village:

SECTION 1. The cemeteries located in the village shall be under the charge of a sexton to be appointed by the board of trustees, and shall be subjected to such rules and regulations as may be prescribed by the board of trustees. **Sexton of cemeteries.**

§ 2. The sexton shall keep the grounds, walks, avenues and streets in the cemeteries in order and free from obstructions. He shall, as often as once in two months, from the fifteenth of April to the sixteenth of November in each year, mow the grass and remove the noxious weeds and thistles from the avenues, streets and walks, and from such surveyed lots as are not properly taken care of by their respective owners, and shall perform such other duties as may be required of him, all under the direction of the cemetery commissioners. It shall be his duty to enforce the ordinances and regulations concerning the cemeteries, he shall have power to arrest all persons trespassing in any manner in the cemeteries, or offending against any provision of the laws of the state or of these ordinances therein, and shall be a special policeman for that purpose. He shall also have power to direct how and where any dead body not belonging to the owner of any lot, shall be buried; and to prevent the deposit of any body in any unsold lot, or in any lot the property of another without the owner's consent. In addition to the duties herein mentioned he shall dig all graves within the grounds of the cemeteries, subject to such regulations as may be prescribed by the ordinances of the village. (Adopted May 28, 1889.) **Duties and powers of sexton.**

Avenues not to be obstructed.

Shrubbery and flowers not to be injured.

Monuments or fences, injury to.

Filth not to be deposited.

§ 3. Any person or persons who shall have any horse or vehicle standing in any avenue, street or path, or who shall fasten or cause to be fastened, any horse in said cemeteries at any other place than at the posts provided for that purpose, or shall cut, break or in other manner destroy any flower, either wild or cultivated, or any herbage, or the fruit or product of any tree, shrub or plant within the cemeteries aforesaid; or shall write upon, soil, deface, remove, displace or in any manner injure or destroy any monument, fence, stake, post or other structure in or belonging to the said cemeteries; or shall deposit or cause to be deposited any filth or unclean or offensive substances in either of the cemeteries or any other place within the village with the intent that the contents thereof should enter said cemeteries; or shall be within the bounds of the Pulteney street or Washington street cemeteries at any time between the hours of eight in evening and six in the morning without permission of the cemetery commissioners, or shall loiter within the bounds of either of said cemeteries and refuse to depart therefrom upon the order of the sexton or any one of the cemetery commissioners, shall be subject to pay a penalty of not less than three nor more than ten dollars for each and every offense. (Adopted May 28, 1889.)

§ 4. Nothing in this chapter is intended to apply to the "Geneva Cemetery Commissioners" who have control and charge of Glenwood cemetery, but is especially applicable to the Pulteney and Washington street cemeteries. (Adopted June 16, 1891.)

CHAPTER VIII.

SHOWS, EXHIBITIONS, CIRCUSES, &C.

Adopted July 24, 1872.

The Trustees of the village of Geneva do enact the following Laws and Ordinances to be observed within the said village:

SECTION 1. Any person who shall exhibit for money any theatrical representations, concerts, caravans, circus, feats of horsemanship, or other natural or artificial curiosity, or any other show, exhibition or performance, shall first obtain a license therefor from the president of the village, for which in no case shall more than fifty dollars be charged for a single exhibition, the amount to be at the discretion of the trustees of the village; and any person who shall violate any of the provisions in this section contained, shall forfeit the sum of fifty dollars, and the further sum of twenty-five dollars for every day he or she may continue such exhibition. (Amended August 20, 1878.)

Circus, theatres, concerts, caravans and shows to be licensed.

§ 2. Licenses shall be granted as aforesaid, upon application therefor and payment of the license fee fixed in each particular case by the president, or by the board of trustees on appeal thereto. The licenses shall specify the object or the length of time for which they have been respectively issued, and shall be subject to the ordinances of the village existing when issued or subsequently passed. It shall be the duty of the person licensed to keep good order in and about his place of exhibition or amusement, and for that purpose to keep at his own expense a sufficient police force.

License fee to be fixed by president or board of trustees.

Exhibitors to provide police and keep order.

§ 3. It shall not be lawful for any person, hereafter, to offer for sale on any of the streets or public places in this village any goods or merchandise of any description, without first obtaining a written license therefor from the

No selling in streets without license.

Clerk of the village, which said license shall be granted only in the discretion of said Clerk and after the payment to him of a fee of ten dollars. Any violation of this ordinance shall subject the offender to a penalty of not less than twenty nor more than fifty dollars. (Adopted July 6, 1886.)

CHAPTER IX.

WEIGHTS AND MEASURES.

Adopted July 24, 1872.

The Trustees of the village of Geneva do enact the following Laws and Ordinances to be observed within the said village:

Sealing weights and measures.

SECTION 1. Any person using weights, measures, scale beams or steelyards, in weighing or measuring any article intended to be purchased or sold in the village, or in the weight or measurement of which other persons or the public are interested, shall cause such weights, measures, scale-beams or steelyards to be sealed and marked by the sealer of weights and measures, and any person who shall neglect or refuse to have the same so sealed and marked, shall be subject to a penalty of five dollars for each offense.

Sealer to have care of public weights, &c.

§ 2. The sealer of weights and measures shall have the care and keeping of the public beam, weights and measures provided for his use, and the same shall be regulated according to the law of the state, and all weights, measures, scale beams and steelyards sealed and adjusted by him, shall be made conformable to the standard of this state; and the said sealer shall, at least once in every six months, and oftener if he deem it necessary, visit the markets, stores, shops or other places where weights, measures, steelyards or beams are kept and used, and examine

To visit markets, &c., every six months—his duties.

the same, and also all measures marked on any counter, desk, seat or other fixture, and in case they be found not agreeable to law, to report the same to the board of trustees. The sealer shall be entitled to ask and receive from the person for whom examination and inspection is performed, such rates as are established by the statutes.

§ 3. The fees aforesaid shall be a lien upon the said weights, measures, beams and scales, and the sealer may sue and prosecute for his services performed under this ordinance in an action in his own name; and for any violation of the provisions of any of the ordinances on this subject, the person so violating shall be liable to the penalties attached, on conviction for the same before the police justice or other magistrate having jurisdiction in the case.

Fees to be a lien.

Penalty for violating sections of this chapter.

§ 4. Any person who shall neglect or refuse to produce any of his weights or measures before the sealer, shall forfeit and pay for the first offense the sum of one dollar; for the second offense five dollars; for the third and every offense thereafter, the sum of ten dollars. It shall be the duty of the sealer to see that all retailers and sellers of milk, beer, ale, cider and vinegar in the village do sell the same by just and true measure, and all offenders in the premises shall be reported by him to the police justice, who shall cause proceedings forthwith to be instituted against such offenders.

Penalty for neglecting or refusing to produce weights and measures.

§ 5. The sealer shall make a regular register of the weights, measures and beams inspected by him, in which he shall record the names of the persons owning the same, and the fact that the same are conformable to the standard of this state; and it shall not be lawful for him to collect the fees mentioned aforesaid more than once in each year, unless the same shall be found on the second examination to be not in conformity with the standard of the state. The sealer shall be entitled to a reasonable compensation for making any beam, weight or measure conform to the established standard. When such beam, weight or meas-

Sealer to make register—his fees, duties, &c.

ure is not conformable to the standard, the scaler shall designate some place in the village where the owner shall send the same to be adjusted, and if the owner shall neglect or refuse so to send them, such owner shall be liable to a penalty of not less than five dollars, and to an additional penalty of two dollars for every twenty-four hours he shall continue such neglect and refusal after conviction for the same.

CHAPTER X.

SALE OF FRESH MEAT AND FISH IN STREETS.

Adopted July 24, 1872.

The Trustees of the village of Geneva do enact the following Law and Ordinance to be observed within the said village:

Fresh fish or meat not to be sold in streets.

SECTION 1. No butcher or other person shall by himself, his agent or servant, expose any fresh fish or any fresh meats of any kind for sale in or upon any of the public squares, streets or alleys of this village except as hereinafter provided, under a penalty of three dollars for every offense.

License for selling in streets.

Any person who shall by himself, his agent or servant, offer for sale any fresh fish or any fresh meats of any kind upon any of the public squares, streets or alleys, shall first obtain a license for such purpose from the president, and pay a fee therefor of not less than two nor more than twenty-five dollars, at the discretion of the board of trustees. No such license shall be granted for a longer time than six months, and may be revoked by the president at any time for proper cause.

Not to apply to farmers.

Nothing in this ordinance contained shall be construed to prevent or hinder any farmer from disposing of his ordinary product of meats, either by the carcass or quarter, but is intended to restrain butchers and other persons from making the streets a daily market place. (Amended April 2, 1878.)

CHAPTER XI.

DOGS.

Adopted July 24, 1872.

The Trustees of the village of Geneva do enact the following Laws and Ordinances to be observed within the said village:

SECTION 1. Any owner or keeper of a dog, bitch or whelp, who shall permit the same to run or be at large contrary to the provisions of this ordinance, shall pay a penalty of five dollars for each offense, and the informer thereof shall be entitled to one-half of said penalty when collected; provided, that nothing in this ordinance shall authorize the destruction of any dog, bitch or whelp found running at large, if such dog, bitch or whelp should be securely muzzled with a wire muzzle, to be fastened on with a leather strap or chain; nor shall a suit be commenced against the owner of any such dog found running at large, securely muzzled as aforesaid. **Dogs not to run at large without muzzle.**

§ 2. It shall and may be lawful for the police constable and the police force of the village, and for any person authorized in writing by the president, to destroy any or all dogs found running at large without a muzzle as aforesaid; and any person who shall molest, interrupt, hinder or prevent the said president, police constable, or persons authorized as herein provided, shall forfeit and pay a penalty in a sum of money not more than twenty-five dollars. **Authority for destroying dogs; penalty for hindering officers.**

CHAPTER XII.

WOOD AND HAY MARKET.

Adopted July 24, 1872.

The Trustees of the village of Geneva do enact the following Laws and Ordinances to be observed within the said village:

Haymarket, where located.

SECTION 1. That part of Castle street east of Linden street shall hereafter be known as "Haymarket," and is hereby designated as the stand for the sale of hay, straw, cornstalks, &c., and loads of hay, straw or cornstalks shall not stand in or upon any other public square, street or alley, exposed for sale. unnder a penalty of five dollars for each offense; and all teams standing in the Haymarket shall stand in such a position as not to obstruct the free travel on either Castle or Water streets, under a penalty of five dollars for each offense.

Stand for wood.

§ 2. Any person exposing wood for sale within this village by the cart, wagon load or sleigh load, shall offer the same upon the Haymarket, and upon no other public square, street or alleys within the village, and upon the place so designated. Any load of wood entering upon said Haymarket designated as the place for the sale of wood, shall be considered as offered or exposed for sale, and shall be at once liable to the provisions of this section.

Measurement of wood.

Any person offering wood for sale shall, at the request of the purchaser, have the same measured by the person appointed by the board of trustees, and his certificate obtained of the amount of wood contained in such load; any refusal to comply with such request shall subject the offender to a penalty of not less than two nor more than ten dollars.

Special charge of wood market.

§ 3. The stand for the sale of wood as aforesaid shall be in the special charge of the wood measurer, the street commissioner and the police constable, and any person who shall violate the provisions of this chapter in regard to locating teams or loads of wood offered for sale, shall be liable to a penalty of two dollars. Any person who shall refuse to locate his team or load as may be required by the wood measurer, the street commissioner or any policeman or other officer of the village, shall be liable to a penalty of two dollars, and a further penalty of two dollars for each hour the load shall remain standing upon the public street or square contrary to such requirements.

CHAPTER XIII.

FIRE LIMITS.

Adopted June 4, 1877.

The Trustees of the village of Geneva do enact the following Law and Ordinance to be observed within the said village:

SECTION 1. The territory within the following boundaries, to wit: beginning at the junction of the centre lines of Main street and Washington street, thence northerly along the centre of Main street to the centre of Colt street; thence eastwardly along the centre of Colt street and said centre line continued to the centre of Geneva street; thence northerly along the centre of Geneva street to centre of Lewis street; thence eastwardly along centre of Lewis street to the east end of the freight depot of the New York Central and Hudson River Rail Road Company; thence south to the centre of Washington street, continued; thence westwardly along the centre of Washington street to the centre of Main street to the place of beginning, is hereby designated and shall be deemed the "Fire Limits" of the village of Geneva, within which "Fire Limits" no person or persons, company, association or

Bounds of fire limits.

Fire proof. buildings to be.

corporation, shall erect, build, put up, or in any manner construct any building or structure, unless the same be built of brick, iron or stone, with slate or metal roof, without the permission of the board of trustees of the village of Geneva, allowing the same.

Penalty.

Any person or persons, company, association or corporation violating this ordinance, shall be subject to and liable to pay a penalty of not less than fifty dollars nor more than two hundred and fifty dollars for each and every violation of the same, to be sued for and recovered in any court of competent jurisdiction.

CHAPTER XIV.

GATES BY RAIL ROAD AT STREET CROSSINGS.

The Trustees of the village of Geneva do enact the following Laws and Ordinances to be observed within said village:

Gates to be placed by rail roads at street crossings.

SECTION 1. On and after the first day of December, 1889, it shall not be lawful for any person, persons or corporation, to cross over or upon any street within the corporate limits of the village of Geneva with any steam railroad engine, or with any cars drawn by such engine, unless the track upon which such crossing is done shall be properly protected by a substantial gate to be built, maintained and operated by and at the expense of the person, persons or corporation so using such track, and such gate shall be closed so as to effectually stop the passage of vehicles at all times during the passing of trains or engines.

Penalty.

§ 2. Any person, persons or corporation violating any of the provisions of the foregoing section shall pay a penalty of not less than twenty-five nor more than fifty dollars for each offense.

§ 3. Nothing in the foregoing sections however shall be so construed as to allow trains, engines or cars to stand upon such crossings so as to obstruct the free use of the streets for travel. (Adopted October 29, 1889.

Cars not to stand on crossings.

CHAPTER XV.

MISCELLANEOUS.

The Trustees of the village of Geneva do enact the following Law and Ordinance to be observed within the said vllage :

SECTION 1. The assessors shall make out all assessment rolls according to the provisions of the sixth section of title four of the village charter, and deliver the same to the board of trustees within twenty days after receiving the order to make out the same, unless otherwise directed by the said board. (Adopted July 24, 1872.)

Assessment roll, when to be delivered.

§ 2. The assessors shall be allowed one hundred dollars each for their services, upon the completion of the assessment roll in the time and manner required by the charter and ordinances of the village, and as they may be required and directed by the board of trustees, said amount to be audited and paid to each assessor, in the discretion of the board of trustees upon a bill rendered and a proper affidavit attached thereto by each of said assessors; and the treasurer shall receive and be paid one hundred dollars per annum for his services. (Adopted June 16, 1891.)

Salary of Assessors.

Salary of treasurer.

§ 3. The president or any trustee is hereby authorized to direct any prosecution to be commenced and prosecuted to judgment against any person in the name of the village of Geneva, for the violation of any law or ordinance of the board of trustees. (Adopted December 8, 1874.)

Any trustee to prosecute for violation of ordinances.

§ 4. The regular and stated meetings of the board of trustees shall be held on Tuesday of each week, at seven o'clock P. M. (Adopted May 4, 1875.)

Meeting of board of trustees.

Pay of street commissioner.

§ 5. The salary of the street commissioner shall be six hundred dollars per year, but the board of trustees may regulate his pay at a fixed rate per diem for actual services performed. (Adopted June 16, 1891.)

Penalty for throwing stones, &c.

§ 6. No person shall throw or cast any stone or other missile, or thing, in, from or to any street, lane, alley, park, public place or unenclosed ground, under a penalty of not less than two nor more than ten dollars. (Adopted November 23, 1875.)

STATE OF NEW YORK, }
ONTARIO COUNTY, } SS.

This is to Certify, That I have compared the foregoing printed copy of the By-Laws and Ordinances of the Trustees of the village of Geneva with the original By-Laws and Ordinances now on record, and that the said By-Laws and Ordinances as contained in this volume from page to page inclusive, are and each is a correct copy of the original, and of the whole of said original. That the same were duly adopted by the Board of Trustees of the village of Geneva at the time and times respectively indicated in the foregoing pages, and that each of said By-Laws and Ordinances were duly published, after their adoption, once in each week for two successive weeks in one of the newspapers published in the village of Geneva, and the same are now in force, and are published by authority of the Board of Trustees of the village of Geneva.

WITNESS MY HAND, and the seal of said village, this day of

Village Clerk.

INDEX TO LAWS AND ORDINANCES.

F

G

H

H

I

K

L

M

N

O

P

P

S

S

PAGE.

T

V

W

www.ingramcontent.com/pod-product-compliance
Lightning Source LLC
Chambersburg PA
CBHW020542270326
41927CB00006B/683